I0088419

SMARTBOOK
GUERRILLA HUNTER KILLER

Contents

		Page
	FOREWORD	i
	PREFACE	v
Chapter 1	GUERRILLA HUNTER KILLER ORDER OF BATTLE	1-1
	Overview	1-1
	Intelligence Preparation of the Battlefield Refresher	1-1
	Taliban Commander	1-1
	Guerrilla Hunter Killer Command and Control	1-1
	External Guerrilla Hunter Killer Command and Control	1-1
	Internal Guerrilla Hunter Killer Command and Control	1-2
	Flexibility	1-2
	Roles and Responsibilities in the Guerrilla Hunter Killer Template	1-2
	Guerrilla Hunter Killer Company	1-2
	Guerrilla Hunter Killer Group	1-4
	Guerrilla Hunter Killer Team	1-5
	Guerrilla Hunter Killer Militia	1-6
Chapter 2	GUERRILLA HUNTER KILLER CIVIL ORGANIZATION	2-1
	Overview	2-1
	Internal Guerrilla Hunter Killer Civil Organization	2-1
	External Guerrilla Hunter Killer Civil Organization	2-1
Chapter 3	GUERRILLA HUNTER KILLER MACRO ZONES	3-1
	Overview	3-1
	Guerrilla Hunter Killer Zone of Operations	3-2
	Guerrilla Hunter Killer Base Camp Zone	3-2
	Guerrilla Hunter Killer Zone of Security	3-2
Chapter 4	GUERRILLA HUNTER KILLER OFFENSIVE OPERATIONS	4-1
	Overview	4-1
	Guerrilla Hunter Killer Offensive Operations	4-1
	Adaptive Operations	4-1
	Purpose of the Offense	4-2
	Attack to Destroy	4-2

Contents

	Attack to Seize	4-2
	Attack to Expel	4-2
	Planned Offense	4-3
	Situational Offense	4-3
	Organizing the Battlefield for the Offense	4-3
	Areas of Responsibility	4-4
	Disruption Zone	4-4
	Battle Zone	4-4
	Forward Support Zone	4-4
	Attack Zone	4-4
	Kill Zone	4-4
Chapter 5	**GUERRILLA HUNTER KILLER DEFENSIVE OPERATIONS**	**5-1**
	Overview	5-1
	Purpose of the Defense	5-1
	Defense to Destroy	5-1
	Defense to Preserve	5-1
	Defense to Deny	5-1
	Planned Defense	5-1
	Situational Defense	5-2
	Areas of Responsibility	5-2
	Disruption Zone	5-2
	Battle Zone	5-3
	Forward Support Zone	5-3
	Attack Zone	5-3
	Kill Zone	5-3
	Battle Position	5-3
	Simple Battle Position	5-4
	Complex Battle Position	5-4
Chapter 6	**CONDITIONS BASED MODEL OF NEEDS**	**6-1**
Chapter 7	**COMPARING THE MODELS**	**7-1**
	The Guerrilla Hunter Killer and The Host Nation Government	5-4
Chapter 8	**THE GUERRILLA HUNTER KILLER OPERATIONAL MODEL**	**8-1**
Chapter 9	**THE HOST NATION OPERATIONAL MODEL**	**9-1**
Chapter 10	**THE GUERRILLA HUNTER KILLER OPERATIONAL CYCLE**	**10-1**
	The Cycle Of Phases	10-1
	Phase 1	10-3
	Phase 2	10-3
	Phase 2a	10-3
	Phase 3	10-3

The Cycle of Phases.

Contents

Chapter 11   **PROCESS FOR DEFINING THE THREAT IN THE DCGS-A MFWS** **11-1**

Create Threat Template... 11-1

Query Data Sources.. 11-1

Create Entities... 11-1

Review Template Against the TED Entities...................................... 11-1

Link Entities to Threat Formations... 11-2

Update Threat Formations... 11-2

Chapter 12   **DATABASES**...**12-1**

Environments.. 12-1

Functions.. 12-1

Analysis... 12-1

Chapter 13   **ENTITY ENVIRONMENTS**..**13-1**

Entity Types... 13-1

Entity Categories... 13-1

Chapter 14   **ENTITY PROPERTY STANDARDS**...**14-1**

Property Fields.. 14-1

Chapter 15   **INTEGRATED FUNCTIONS WITHIN 5/2 SBCT OPERATIONS**...........................**15-1**

Making Intelligence History in Afghanistan..................................... 15-1

Why Is Full Integration Important... 15-2

Central Information Repository for All To Utilize............................. 15-3

Garbage In, garbage Out... 15-4

Chapter 16   **MFWS ENTITY STANDARDS**..**16-1**

MFWS System Field Configuration... 16-1

Check Fields In Quickforms Setup.. 16-2

Chapter 17   **MFWS DATA ENTRY FORMATTING**..**17-1**

Equipment Entity...17-1

Vehicle Entity.. 17-1

Facility Entity...17-2

Place Entity..17-2

Organization Entity.. 17-3

Person Entity... 17-3

Person Entity (Continued).. 17-4

Event Entity... 17-4

Financial Transaction Entity.. 17-5

Financial Transaction Entity (Continued)... 17-5

Chapter 18   **COMMON PROPERTY STANDARDS**...**18-1**

Common Properties... 18-1

Address Property... 18-1

Communications Property.. 18-1

Criminal History Property.. 18-2

Skills Property.. 18-2

Rules For Recording Analyst Block Entries...................................... 18-3

Settings For Entity Fields.. 18-4

Settings For Entity Fields (Continued)... 18-5

Persistent Jabber Chat... 18-6
SOURCE NOTES .... SOURCE NOTES-1
SOURCE NOTES .... SOURCE NOTES-2
GLOSSARY GLOSSARY-1
GLOSSARY GLOSSARY-2
GLOSSARY GLOSSARY-3
GLOSSARY GLOSSARY-4
SYMBOLOGY SYMBOLOGY-1
AFTERWORD.. ix

FIGURES

Figure 1-1. Guerrilla Hunter Killer Company....................................... 1-2
Figure 1-2. Guerrilla Hunter Killer Group.. 1-4
Figure 1-3. Guerrilla Hunter Killer Team... 1-5
Figure 3-1. Guerrilla Hunter Killer Macro Zones.................................3-1
Figure 4-1. Guerrilla Hunter Killer AORs in the Offense.................... 4-3
Figure 5-1. Guerrilla Hunter Killer AORs in the Defense.................... 5-1
Figure 5-2. Battle Positions.. 5-4
Figure 6-1a. Maslow's Hierarchy of Needs...6-1
Figure 6-1b. Conditions Based Hierarchy... 6-1
Figure 7-1. Comparison of the GH/K and the Host Nation Operational Model 7-1
Figure 8-1. Guerrilla Hunter Killer Operational Model.......................8-1
Figure 9-1. The Host Nation Operational Model................................ 9-1
Figure 10-1. The Cycle of Phases.. 10-1

Foreword

The 572nd Military Intelligence Company, in conjunction with the brigade's Intelligence War Fighting Function, set the standard for accurately and effectively defining the environment during our Counter-Insurgency campaign in Southern Afghanistan. Their efforts enabled me to make informed decisions about the allocation of resources and employment of maneuver forces on the battlefield to protect the populace, counter the threat, and protect the force.

The multi-national composition of Regional Command South (RC-S) made establishing standards for intelligence operations, with its inherent processes and procedures, difficult. The Regional Command and our coalition partners were constrained by the lack of a pre-established standard for data management, information flow, and intelligence process. These constraints resulted in the inability to establish a regional common intelligence picture for Southern Afghanistan to consolidate knowledge across each subordinate task force. Our Area of Operations contained a myriad of intelligence organizations from numerous nations, operating on different data networks using disparate analytic tools. The Guerrilla Hunter Killer Smartbook was built on a doctrinal foundation combined with historical studies of Guerrilla Warfare and details the methods used to standardize the intelligence process at the Brigade Combat Team and below. This book provides the tactical intelligence professional with a doctrinal based reference outlining how 5/2 ID (SBCT) defined the battlespace, streamlined our intelligence process to improve the ability for Commander's to make decision across the brigade.

The brigade's Intelligence War Fighting Function standardized its practices using Army Battle Command Systems (ABCS) to produce comprehensive Area Intelligence products and assessments using the Army's Intelligence Analysis tool, the Distributed Common Ground System – Army (DCGS-A). Through the various intelligence, operational, and civil military data sets available to the DCGS-A system, our analysts were able to accurately define the environment to facilitate deliberate and rapid decision making throughout the brigade's area of operation.

The Guerrilla Hunter Killer Smartbook is extremely valuable for both intelligence professionals and maneuver commanders conducting counter-insurgency operations. This book provides a framework, validated through execution, as a foundation and for transforming an overwhelming amount of data into a comprehensive picture of the environment and its components. I believe this work helps to bridge the gap between the "art" and "science" of Military Intelligence by outlining a clear methodology for producing intelligence while waging a Counter-Insurgency Campaign.

HARRY D. TUNNELL IV
COL, IN
Commanding

Preface

Recently President Barrack Obama authorized 30,000 additional troops be sent to Afghanistan over the course of twelve months to support General McCrystal's comprehensive Counter-Insurgency (COIN) strategy for Afghanistan. This new approach to the war in Afghanistan is meant to focus on providing greater security for the people of Afghanistan, discrediting the Taliban and helping to train Afghanistan's security forces. This is a sound strategy and the additional forces will certainly help improve the situation in Afghanistan. However, additional attention must be given to the biggest shortcoming in either Afghanistan or Iraq; Once again allowing Military Intelligence to drive Maneuver. In order for intelligence to drive maneuver we must — 1) understand and define the enemy we face and how he fights and 2) capture the various data streams of information across all intelligence disciplines, and turn this raw data into comprehensive, fused intelligence assessments using a common set of tools. This "Smartbook" is a compilation of the Tactics, Techniques and Procedures that the 572nd Military Intelligence Company used during OEF 09-11 to provide timely and accurate intelligence products and assessments to the brigade and subordinate battalions of 5th Brigade, 2nd Infantry Division (Stryker Brigade Combat Team).

Methodology

After realizing that personality based targeting efforts were often times futile and counterproductive, we opted to focus on producing "Area Intelligence" instead. Our approach to Area Intelligence consisted of three main components; Area Fusion Teams (the structure that makes area intelligence possible), DCGS-A (the tool), and the Guerrilla Hunter Killer (Threat Template).

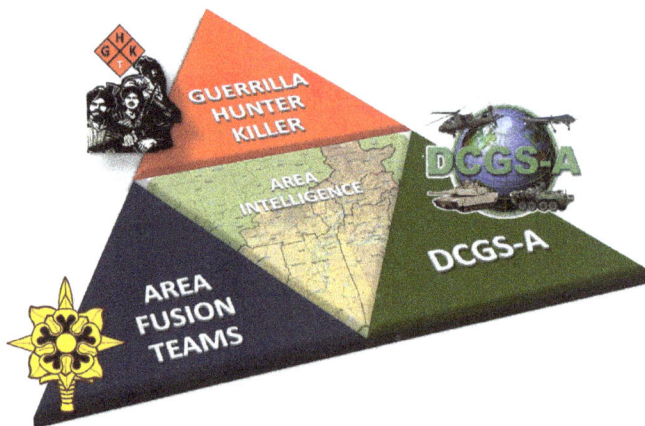

Area Intelligence

The unconventional battlefield is an often times chaotic and confusing environment which pushes modern intelligence analysts beyond what most of their training has taught them. Analysts can no longer focus on just targeting and removing specific individuals from the battlefield, which has been the focus of efforts both in Iraq and Afghanistan, but instead must account for several varying factors to develop a holistic assessment of the area of operations to clearly and accurately define the operational environment. Mao Tse Tung described his war of resistance against the Japanese as a "war of jigsaw pattern[i]." By this he meant that the battlefield, "instead of a pattern of definable

Preface

front lines, as in conventional warfare, Mao's war of resistance would be broken into many tiny bits each containing its own separate "mini-war." Mao envisioned that some of the jigsaw pieces would be "safe" for his movement and others "safe" for his opponents, but the greatest number of pieces would be contested to some extent by both sides[ii]." Knowing the numerous sources of information available, and the ineffectiveness of personality based targeting we made a shift towards Area Intelligence. G.L. Lamborn defined it best by stating that, "It [Area Intelligence] identifies which districts, villages or hamlets actively assist the insurgents, which villages cooperate under duress with the insurgents, and which areas are generally supportive of the government-in-being. But not only does Area Intelligence identify local allegiances, it strives to give the underlying reasons for those allegiances[iii]." Analysts must now take into account ethnic and tribal dynamics, corruption, projects (both NGO and military initiated), and local security forces operations in conjunction with their effectiveness (or in-effectiveness), Human Terrain Team (HTT) data, and the enemy situation to form accurate assessments and paint the "jigsaw puzzle" that is the unconventional battlefield for commanders. Providing true Area Intelligence will produce the comprehensive picture maneuver commanders and staffs require to adequately assign resources to areas and form the basis for a solid, effective maneuver plan.

Area Fusion Team

The various intelligence disciplines can no longer be separated from one another, producing stovepipes of intelligence. Instead they must work together, fusing the intelligence disciplines together at every step. Our solution, based on the need to fuse the various forms of intelligence in order to make true All-Source, Area Intelligence assessments, came in the form of creating Area Fusion Teams (AFT). The AFTs were assigned an Area of Operations (AO) for which they provide intelligence oversight. Each team generally consisted of: one AFT leader, a 35F20 All Source Analyst who provides the direction and immediate oversight of intelligence analysis; one 35F10 whose main responsibility is to data mine and process reports and one 35N Signals Intelligence (SIGINT) Analyst who provides on the spot SIGINT analysis for collaboration with the all source analysts. The AFTs interacted directly with the company's Collection Management and Dissemination Cell (CM&D), Imagery Intelligence (IMINT) and Measures and Signatures Intelligence (MASINT) sections as required to further fuse the intelligence disciplines.

DCGS-A

The Distributive Common Ground System-Army (DCGS-A) is what the brigade was fielded and expected to use as the primary means to collect, process, and analyze battlefield information into analytical products for the brigade commander. The DCGS-A program was developed in order to "pass critical information and intelligence down to the level required[iv]," and "by design breaks stovepipe data barriers, alters collaboration methods, and enhances the Brigade Combat Team Commander's ability to ACT on actionable intelligence[v]." Recognizing the advertised capabilities of DCGS-A, we took the tool and made it work, where the Army's Flagship tool failed to be integrated into other intelligence processes. We pushed the system to its full capabilities, proving that DCGS-A does support the intelligence process at the Brigade Combat Team level.

The Guerrilla Hunter Killer

To effectively defeat an enemy, one must first understand the enemy. Intelligence professionals have forgotten the basic principles on which intelligence analysis is conducted, instead they subscribe to the paradigm that the enemy faced in this Global War on Terror has no structure or doctrine. Any organization, military or civilian, must have a structure and a way of doing business if they are to have any chance of being successful. As previously stated, understanding an enemy is critical to defeating him, but how much do we really understand the Taliban? We know that the Taliban fights in small groups using unconventional tactics that usually manifest themselves in the form of Improvised Explosive Device (IED), Direct Fire (DF), and Indirect Fire (IDF) attacks against Coalition Forces (CF) vehicles, patrols, and operating bases. The Taliban uses fear and intimidation against the Afghan people, collecting taxes, establishing court systems based on Shari'a law and doling out justice when these laws are broken. We also know that the Taliban enjoys sanctuary in regions bordering Afghanistan, such as Pakistan, with most of their senior leadership issuing decrees and orders just across the border. All of these "knowns" about the Taliban are not new to warfare of this nature, instead many of these same factors have been observed all over the world and throughout time. The military leader and fighter Ernesto "Che" Guevara waged guerrilla campaigns in multiple countries almost forty years ago using many of the same tactics the Taliban employ today. Che's successful war in Cuba and his failed guerrilla movements in the Congo and Bolivia are not the only historical examples of low intensity conflict that resemble our current fight in Afghanistan. Mao Tse Tung, Carlos Marighella and Alberto Bayo are just a few other Guerrilla leaders whose writings were examined and captured in the Guerrilla Hunter Killer Template. Volumes of source documents exist that can be referenced to help understand and define the enemy. Interestingly, the Guerrilla Hunter Killer Template was written using these source documents almost exclusively, but as you will see the parallels to the Taliban are frightening and therefore applicable to the war in Afghanistan. Truly understanding and defining the enemy as a collective group, not as individuals, is key to defeating him. The GH/K template blends historical writings of Guerrilla Leaders in conjunction with current and past United States Army doctrine to form the "melting pot" that is The Guerrilla Hunter Killer.

Once a base line understanding of the enemy was established, we understood the need to use common graphics and terms to accurately describe the enemy formations and tactical tasks. Simply using U.S. Army operational terms and graphics does a severe disservice to all involved. The enemy we face is not the U.S. Army, and we should not attempt to "make them fit" into our own maneuver doctrine. While some tactical terms and graphics may fit what the enemy is trying to accomplish and how he organizes himself a majority do not, and at the end of the day this method is simply shoe horning the enemy into doctrine meant for ourselves. The enemy deserves his own graphics and tactical terms, for his structure and tasks are unique to what he is attempting to accomplish.

---

[i] Mao Tse-tung, "On Protracted War," Selected Military Writings, p. 219.
[ii] The *People in Arms, A Practitioner's Guide to Understanding Insurgency And dealing with it effectively* by G.L. Lamborn
[iii] The *People in Arms, A Practitioner's Guide to Understanding Insurgency And dealing with it effectively* by G.L. Lamborn.
[iv] S-2 Guide for Distributed Common Ground System (DCGS A); September 30, 2009.
[v] S-2 Guide for Distributed Common Ground System (DCGS A); September 30, 2009.

Chapter 1
Guerrilla Hunter Killer Order of Battle

"In the Sierra Maestra, a communist leader who visited us, admiring such Improvisation and how all the little details being worked out separately were adjusted to centralized organization, stated that it was the most perfectly organized chaos in the universe."

Ernesto "Che" Guevara's letter to Ernesto Sabato, April 12, 1960
Episodes of the Cuban Revolutionary War, 1956-1958

This chapter discusses the order of battle templates derived and used by 5/2 ID (SBCT) to help define the threat faced in our Area of Operations (AO). The name and basic organization come from FM 7-100.4 (Opposing Force Organization Guide) with some slight modification to more accurately reflect the current enemy structure[1].

1-1. Intelligence Preparation of the Battlefield Refresher.

Intelligence Preparation of the Battlefield (IPB) is a systematic process that builds upon itself. Without seriously considering step three (Evaluate the Threat) one cannot move on to step four (Determine Threat Course of Action). Attempting to understand how the enemy organizes and fights allows intelligence analysts to get back to predictive analysis; allowing commanders at all levels to make more informed decisions and allowing intelligence to once again drive maneuver. Once a baseline understanding is established, ISR assets can be employed to confirm or deny the initial assessment. ISR confirmation will not only provide greater clarity to enemy formations and their mission, but it will also drive targeting efforts for commanders. Accurate targeting enables offensive operations as opposed to movement to contact.

1-2. Taliban Commander.

A common case of not using precise terms precisely for Afghanistan can be found in the following example—Mullah X is a TB Commander operating in Zabul and Mullah Y is a TB Commander operating in Arghandab. Both Mullahs are defined as Taliban Commanders, but Mullah X operating in Zabul commands 20 fighters, while Mullah Y operating in Arghandab commands only 5 fighters. Applying the Guerrilla Hunter Killer (GH/K) template; Mullah X is a GH/K Group leader operating in Zabul and Mullah Y is a GH/K Team leader operating in Arghandab. If one understands and uses the GH/K template a general understanding of the actual number of forces commanded is clear. Using the Guerrilla Hunter Killer (GH/K) template alleviates vagueness and interpretation while supporting the decision making process for the allocation of resources and assets for maneuver commanders.

1-3. Guerrilla Hunter Killer Command and Control.

Due to the unique nature of Guerrilla Hunter Killer operations, Command and Control (C2) of the Guerrilla Hunter Killer can be expressed and understood as external and internal. Both are unique in their organization and tasks they are responsible for accomplishing as part of the overall GH/K end state.

1-4. External Guerrilla Hunter Killer Command and Control.

External GH/K C2 (EGH/K C2)[2] is part of the GH/K structure but is not located within the principal GH/K Macro Zones, but is instead located in a neighboring country or state not actively involved in GH/K Operations. External GH/K C2 will develop the left and right limits of GH/K operations and organization along with issuing broad guidance to Internal GH/K C2. External GH/K C2 will supply Internal GH/K C2 with supplies not readily available within the principal GH/K zones.

1-5. Internal Guerrilla Hunter Killer Command and Control.

Internal GH/K C2 (IGH/K C2)[3] comes from GH/K units located in the principal GH/K Macro Zones. The internal GH/K C2 acts independently with minimal guidance from the External GH/K C2. When given a specific task by the External GH/K C2 this task will take preference, otherwise the Internal GH/K C2 displays its own initiative by planning and executing their own actions along with the procurement of logistics easily obtainable in zone.

1-6. Flexibility.

While the GH/K template is expressed in a line and block format, the template is not as rigid as one may assume. The intent is not to build a Soviet- style Order of Battle. The intent instead is to provide a starting point for intelligence analysts and commanders to better understand and visualize the enemy. Fully understanding the enemy is the key to effective targeting, separation from the population and eventual defeat of enemy forces. All echelons of the GH/K may shrink or expand for certain AO's. This is not a "one-size-fits-all" approach or solution.

1-7. Roles and Responsibility in the Guerrilla Hunter Killer Template.

Key to understanding the GH/K concept is the fact that one individual may be responsible for one or more roles depicted on the GH/K template. The template is just a starting point to visually depict these roles, and remind analysts and commanders that certain roles are essential for the Guerrilla Hunter Killer to be successful and accomplish his mission.

1-8. Guerrilla Hunter Killer Company[4].

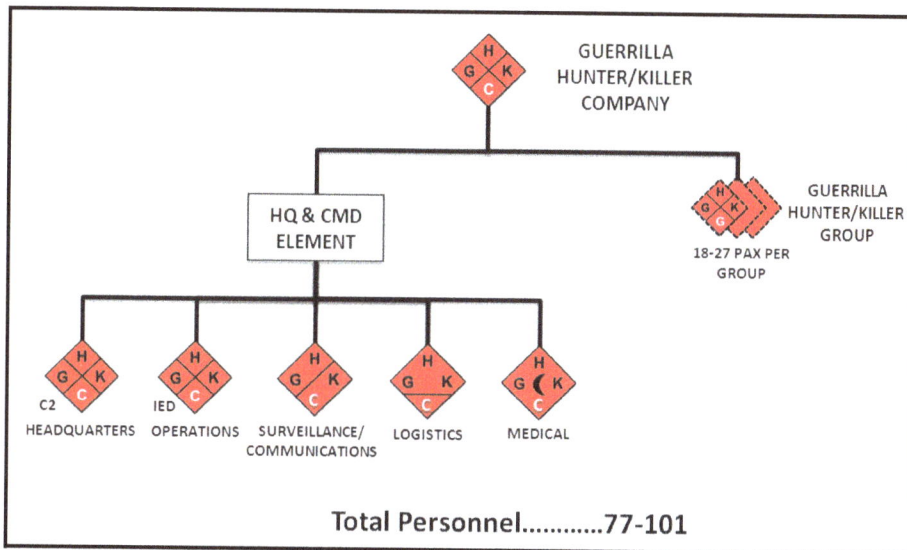

Figure 1-1. Guerrilla Hunter Killer Company.

Overview. The GH/K Company has anywhere from 77-101 personnel comprised of 3 GH/K Groups and a Headquarters and Command element. The GH/K Company Headquarters and Command element is responsible for providing command and control as well as logistical support for GH/K Group operations. The GH/K Company is assessed to exist at the District level, while most GH/K Operations take place below the Provincial level.

a. **C2.** The GH/K Company Commander will be the interface with the External GH/K C2. A GH/K Company Commander and Deputy provide broad guidance, based on EGH/K C2, to GH/K Group Commanders as well as ensure GH/K Groups have all of the necessary logistical support to conduct operations.

b. **IED Operations.** At the GH/K Company level IED Operations personnel will assembly the most raw of materials into IED components to be used at the GH/K Group IED Operations level. It is at this level that the most comprehensive explosive knowledge will exist. Home Made Explosive (HME) will be made at this level, as well as the procurement of electronics to be used in IEDs. This may include the importation of IED materials from Pakistan.

c. **Surveillance/Communications.** Dedicated to providing Early Warning (EW). Makes extensive use of the civilian populace.

Chapter 1

d. **Logistics.** GH/K Company Logisticians are responsible for obtaining weapons and vehicles for GH/K Groups as well as delivery to the various GH/K Groups.

e. **Medical.** Medical care at the GH/K Company level is the most comprehensive available. Medical staff at the GH/K Company level will have formal medical training and be active GH/K supporters. At this level the medical personnel will work solely for the GH/K, as opposed to medical personnel at the GH/K Group level who may primarily work at civilian hospitals or clinics.

1-9. Guerrilla Hunter Killer Group[5].

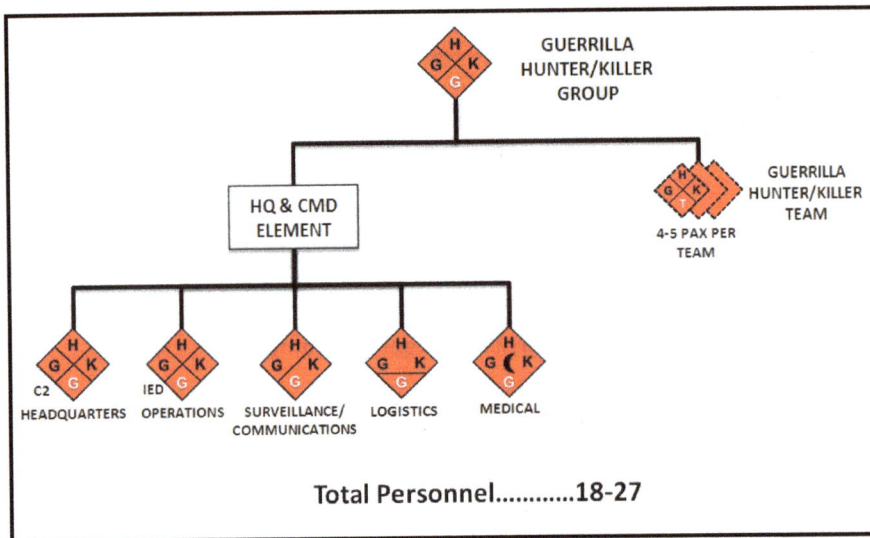

Figure 1-2. Guerrilla Hunter Killer Group.

Overview. GH/K Groups will have anywhere from 18-27 personnel comprised of three GH/K Teams and a Headquarters and Command element. The GH/K Group Headquarters and Command element is responsible for providing command and control as well as logistical support for GH/K Team operations. It is assessed that multiple GH/K Groups will operate within a district. The GH/K group was commonly the largest formation that conducted operations in the Task Force Stryker AO.

a. **C2.** The GH/K Group Leader takes broad guidance from the GH/K Company Commander and executes operations. The GH/K Group leader will communicate with other GH/K Group Leaders if support is needed in the form of men or material and to synchronize efforts. A GH/K Group Deputy is a possibility but not a necessity for the GH/K Group to be successful.

UNCLASSIFIED

b. **IED Operations.** IED materials are received from the GH/K Company level, and are assembled almost to completion for distribution to the GH/K Team for emplacement.

c. **Surveillance/Communications.** Surveillance at the GH/K Group level help GH/K Group Leaders plan their movement without Coalition Forces (CF) detection, plan deliberate operations as well as exploit targets of opportunity. Civilians are a key component of GH/K reconnaissance efforts; however they are not depicted on the template. Civilians acting in a reconnaissance effort are most likely GH/K Contact, sympathizers, or may support GH/K efforts due to intimidation.

d. **Logistics.** Responsible for coordinating with the GH/K Company Logistics section for materials necessary to conduct operations.

e. **Medical.** Medical support at the GH/K Group level will have some medical training, but not necessarily as formal training as the GH/K Company Medical Personnel. The GH/K Group medical personnel will take full advantage of civilian medical facilities and personnel. The medical staff providing support at civilian medical facilities will not be active GH/K supporters.

1-10. Guerrilla Hunter Killer Team[6].

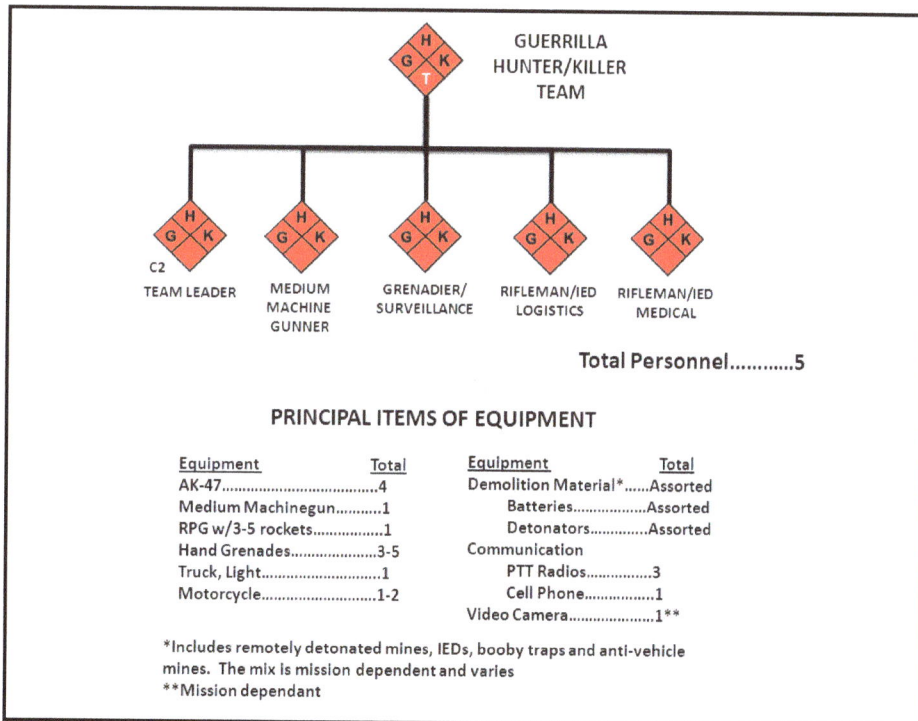

Figure 1-3. Guerrilla Hunter Killer Team.

Overview. The GH/K Team is the most effective unit in the Guerrilla Hunter Killer formation[7] and the most commonly seen unit on the battlefield. The GH/K Team recognizes it is subordinate to the GH/K Group and will execute direct orders from the GH/K Group but mostly the GH/K Team will operate under its own initiative. This includes selecting their own targets and being responsible for basic logistical needs[8]. A member of the GH/K Team may be assigned more than one role in the Team. For example a specific mission may not call for the Grenadier to employ his RPG or ammunition for the RPG may not be available, therefore he may take on the role of surveillance for the GH/K Team.

a. **C2/Team Leader.** The GH/K Team Leader is responsible for executing GH/K operations within the Guerrilla Hunter Killer Zone of Operations. The GH/K Team Leader will display the upmost initiative in conducting operations in his assigned zone, and usually operates with little to no guidance from the GH/K Group level.
- Medium Machine Gunner
- Grenadier/Surveillance
- Rifleman/IED/Logistics
- Rifleman/IED/Medical

1-11. Guerrilla Hunter Killer Militia[9].

Overview. The Guerrilla Hunter Killer must have the support of the local population in order to be effective, therefore Guerrilla Hunter Killer Militia's in rural villages and hamlets may be organized under local leadership. This is one of the GH/K's most effective methods of extending control over the local population and insuring their support. Civilians, organized and committed to an active part of the Guerrilla Hunter Killer movement are more inclined to provide support to the GH/K forces and less likely to turn to the enemy.

b. **Composition.** The Guerrilla Hunter Killer Militia will be formed out of pre-existing village "home guards" if available, otherwise the GH/K Militia will be formed out of able bodied men sympathetic to the Guerrilla Hunter Killer movement. The size of the GH/K Militia will vary depending on the size of their respective village, but the GH/K Militia will be structurally as close to GH/K main forces organization as possible, and will not exceed typical GH/K Group size.

c. **Role and Responsibility.** The GH/K Militia is not primarily designed to be a mobile fighting force, but instead a "back up," and supplement for the better trained and equipped main GH/K forces. GH/K Militias can perform many of the same functions as the GH/K Team, e.g. Improvised Explosive Device (IED) emplacement and Small Arms Fire (SAF) ambushes. In addition the GH/K Militia can provide intelligence collection for main GH/K forces in the form of enemy troop concentrations and movements, locals cooperating with the enemy and an invaluable knowledge of the terrain in their respective zone. Guerrilla Hunter Killer Militia's can also be used to disseminate GH/K propaganda to further attain support for main GH/K forces operating in the zone.

d. Command and Control. The GH/K Militia will be under local leadership, but is always subordinate to the main Guerrilla Hunter Killer Forces operating in the zone. The GH/K Militia will fall under either the Internal or External Guerrilla Hunter Killer Civil Organization explained in the next chapter.

1-12. Guerrilla Hunter Killer Contact[10].

a. Overview. Because the GH/K relies heavily on the support of the local populace in the GH/K Zones, there will be segments of the local population that provide key functions for the GH/K. These functions include but are not limited to movement of GH/K personnel, supplies, storage of weapons and ammunition, information on enemy troop movements, information on informers, acting as guides and couriers between GH/K formations. Motivations can vary for the GH/K Contact. These motivations can be monetary, ideological, fear or a combination of all three. The GH/K Contact will not be a participant in GH/K direct action, nor will the GH/K allow it for the GH/K requires that the Contact is able to move freely through the various zones amongst the people, Guerrilla's and enemy forces.

Chapter 2
Guerrilla Hunter Killer Civil Organization

It is the ultimate goal of the overall Guerrilla Hunter Killer organization to replace an existing government with their own. Therefore the GH/K must have a civil organization component to effectively govern the local populace of a given area as more territory falls under GH/K control[11].

2-1. Internal Guerrilla Hunter Killer Civil Organization.
The Internal Guerrilla Hunter Killer Civil Organization (IGH/KCO) is found in the GH/K Base Camp Zone. The IGH/KCO is emplaced to efficiently govern the local populace and influence the people to the GH/K's side. The functions of the internal IGH/KCO can include, but are not limited to collection of taxes, establishment of a penal code and civil code along with the establishment of a judicial system to settle local disputes and enforce punishment on the local population for failure to follow the established IGH/KCO laws. The IGH/KCO will also establish regulations for the population to contribute food and other necessary supplies to the GH/K. There will always be a strong propaganda element to the IGH/KCO IOT explain to the population the reasons for the implementation of taxes and laws. This propaganda will also show how the legitimate government is not providing the basic civil functions where as the IGH/KCO is. Through this propaganda the GH/K will be able to exploit their success amongst the local population in other zones enabling the further penetration of the GH/K for the GH/K's success lies in the support of the people.

2-2. External Guerrilla Hunter Killer Civil Organization.
The External Guerrilla Hunter Killer Civil Organization (EGH/KCO) is found in the Zone of Security and Operations. The EGH/KCO performs many of the same functions as the IGH/KCO but is nowhere near as robust as the IGH/KCO because these zones are not under full GH/K control.

This page intentionally left blank.

Chapter 3
Guerrilla Hunter Killer Macro Zones

The primary mission of the Guerrilla Hunter Killer is to continually expand his control over a country or state. In order to accomplish this mission, the battlefield can viewed from a Macro level as comprising three primary zones. Each zone performs a specific function to the Guerrilla Hunter Killer and are necessary to expand his control[12]. Defining and understanding the battlefield using these zones can be used as a clear measure of effectiveness for maneuver forces over time.

3-1. Macro Level Guerrilla Hunter Killer Zones.

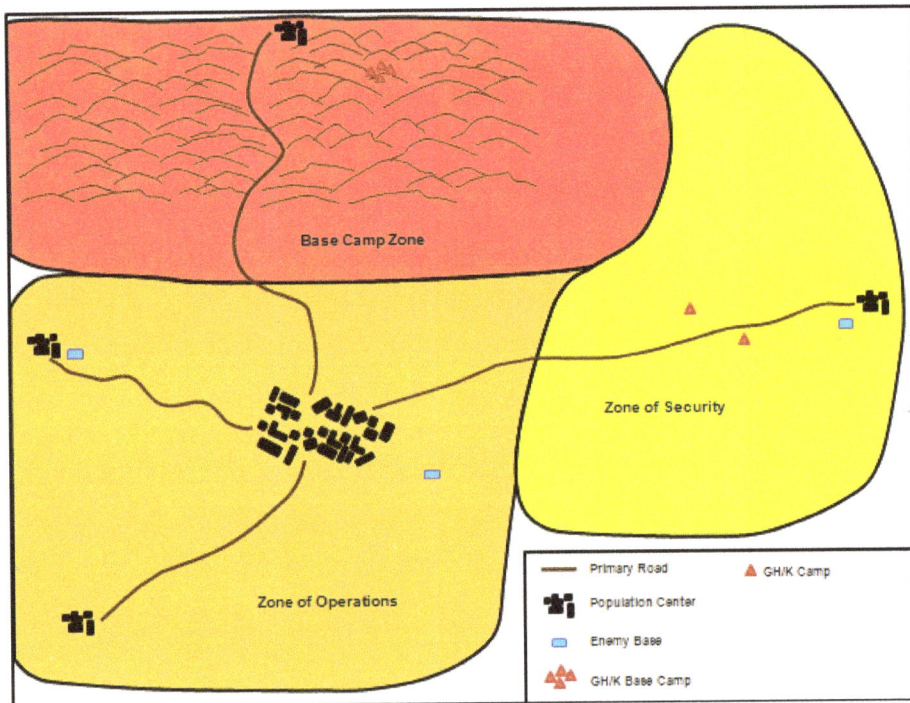

Figure 3-1. Guerrilla Hunter Killer Macro Zones.

3-2. Guerrilla Hunter Killer Zone of Operations[13].

This is the principal zone of GH/K operations, as it is somewhat effectively controlled by the enemy. GH/K's seek to bring more and more of this zone under effective control. The Zone of Operations can further be divided into the Guerrilla Hunter Killer Micro (below) zones among the subordinate GH/K units. Within these areas each subordinate unit exercises control over the civilian population, selects targets and carries out attacks with broad guidance from their next level of command. Occasionally the GH/K will be directed to carry out a specific attack which will take precedence, but this is not the norm. The GH/K Micro Zone definitions will be explained in more detail in Chapters 4 and 5.

- Battle Zone
- Attack Zone
- Kill Zone
- Disruption Zone
- Forward Support Zone

3-3. Guerrilla Hunter Killer Base Camp Zone[14].

This zone is effectively controlled by the Guerrilla Hunter Killer. Headquarters and base camps will be located in this zone, usually in difficult terrain. Limited defensive operations will be conducted in this zone against enemy forces seeking to penetrate this zone.

a. Guerrilla Hunter Killer Base Camps[15]. Located within the Base Camp Zone, GH/K Base Camps house command posts, training areas, communications facilities, medical stations, and logistics centers. The Guerrilla Hunter Killer can defend or attack out of his GH/K base camp. However, it is important to note that the GH/K does not seek to defend these base camps for any length of time; therefore he does not employ fixed, contiguous defensive fronts. The GH/K will only defend for a short time, as part of a larger movement out of the area.

b. Characteristics of a Guerrilla Hunter Killer base camp[16].

- Cover and concealment.
- Rough, inaccessible terrain.
- Suitable for bivouac
- Remoteness

3-4. Guerrilla Hunter Killer Zone of Security[17].

This zone is not controlled effectively by either the Guerrilla Hunter Killer or the enemy. This is the principal transient area used by the GH/K to reach the Zone of Operations. The GH/K will not offer determined resistance to the enemy in this zone for he wishes to keep this zone open in order to maintain freedom of maneuver from the Base Camp Zone to the Zone of Operations and vice versa. The GH/K will conduct limited harassing type attacks to limit enemy movement in the zone.

a. Guerrilla Hunter Killer camp. The GH/K camp is a small temporary position employed by the GH/K in the Zone of Security in route to the Zone of Operations or Base Camp Zone. The GH/K camp is employed for resting of forces, intermediate C2 or sudden meetings of GH/K leadership.

Chapter 4
Guerrilla Hunter Killer Offensive Operations

"The contemporary operational environment (COE) is the overall operational environment that exists today and in the near future (out to the year 2020). The range of threats during this period extends from smaller, lower-technology opponents using more adaptive, asymmetric methods to larger, modernized forces able to engage deployed U.S. forces in more conventional, symmetrical ways. In some possible conflicts (or in multiple, concurrent conflicts), a combination of these types of threats could be especially problematic."

OEF TACTICS, TECHNIQUES AND PROCEDURES HANDBOOK. 02-8

As previously mentioned, we cannot attempt to make operational terms and graphics meant to describe U.S. Army operations fit our enemy's intentions. Therefore a new set of language must be used to illustrate what enemy commanders and formations are trying to achieve. The COE was designed just for that purpose. COE must be understood and used at all levels in order to be effective. The main source consulted to define GH/K operations was FM 7-100.1 (OPFOR Operations).

4-1. Guerrilla Hunter Killer Offensive Operations[18].
The Guerrilla Hunter Killer sees the offensive as the decisive form of operations and the ultimate means of imposing its will on the enemy. While conditions at a particular time or place may require the GH/K to defend, these defensive operations are only conducted to allow the GH/K to exfiltrate back to a more secure zone. GH/K Defensive operations will be covered later on in this chapter. GH/K commanders at all levels seek to create and exploit opportunities to take offensive action, whenever possible.

4-2. Adaptive Operations.
Once the Guerrilla Hunter Killer occupies a zone traditionally considered free from GH/K forces, the GH/K does not avoid battle. He seeks it often, but on its own terms. Battles will occur at a place and time of the GH/K's choosing IOT maximize the GH/K strengths and minimize his weakness.

"The more uncomfortable the guerrilla fighter is, and the more he is initiated into the rigours of nature, the more he feels at home; his morale is higher; his sense of security greater...He has learned to risk his life...to trust it to luck like a tossed coin...It matters little to the individual guerrilla whether or not he survives."

Ernesto "Che" Guevara

a. When the GH/K can create a window of opportunity or exploit opportunity created by natural conditions that limit or degrade enemy capabilities, its forces move out of their Base Camp Zones and Zones of Security. They try to force the enemy to operate in areas where GH/K operations can be most effective. The GH/K uses windows of opportunity to destroy key enemy systems or cause mass casualties.

4-3. Purpose of the Offense.

The purpose of any given GH/K offensive operation varies with the situation. The primary distinction among types of offensive operations is their purpose. Thus, the GH/K recognizes three general types of offensive operations according to their purpose: to destroy, seize, or expel.

4-4. Attack to Destroy.

An attack to destroy is designed to eliminate a target entity as a useful fighting force. Attacks to destroy usually focus on key enemy combat formations or capabilities. Not every soldier or system needs to be destroyed for such an attack to be successful. Attacks to destroy are often focused on a single component of an enemy's combat system. For example, it may be enough for a GH/K to remove one combat vehicle from an enemy formation, or cause casualties. The GH/K realizes that attacks to destroy, even with seemingly minimal impacts to the enemy combat power still carry with them a severe impact to enemy morale and will to fight. These attacks also show the local population that the GH/K can engage and destroy a numerically superior force at a place and time of the GH/K's choosing, discrediting any enemy counter-insurgency efforts to provide security to the local population. Attacks to destroy often have a strong information warfare component (IW).

4-5. Attack to Seize.

An attack to seize is designed to gain control of a key terrain feature or man-made facility. While attacks to seize are not norm for the GH/K, he still maintains the ability to conduct such attacks if the situation arises. One example may be a GH/K group conducting an attack to seize a prison facility IOT free imprisoned GH/K members[19].

4-6. Attack to Expel.

An attack to expel is used to force the defender to vacate an area. Attacks to expel often have a strong IW component like an attack to destroy, so that the enemy removes himself from the area largely through a loss of resolve. Attacks to expel typically focus on a key enemy capability or vulnerability, and can be considered to be the overall mission of the higher echelons of the GH/K. For example the GH/K Company may be conducting an Attack to Expel, but the mission at the GH/K Group and Team level would be an attack to destroy.

Planning Offensive Operations.
4-7. Planned Offense.
A planned (deliberate) offense is an offensive operation or action undertaken when there is suffi-cient time and knowledge of the situation to prepare and rehearse forces for specific tasks. Typi-cally, the enemy is in prepared defensive positions and in a known location. Key considerations in offensive planning are-
• Selecting a clear and appropriate objective
• Developing a reconnaissance plan that locates and tracks relevant enemy targets and elements
• Determining which component or components of an enemy's combat system to attack.

4-8. Situational Offense.
The GH/K realizes that the modern battlefield is chaotic. Fleeting opportunities to attack an enemy weakness continually present themselves and just as quickly disappear. Therefore the GH/K nor-mally will conduct a situational (hasty) offense. Having pre-established battle drills by GH/K Groups and Teams as well as pre-assembled and pre-emplaced Improvised Explosive Devices (IED) help GH/K commanders to take advantage of these fleeting opportunities on the battlefield.

Organizing the Battlefield for the Offense.

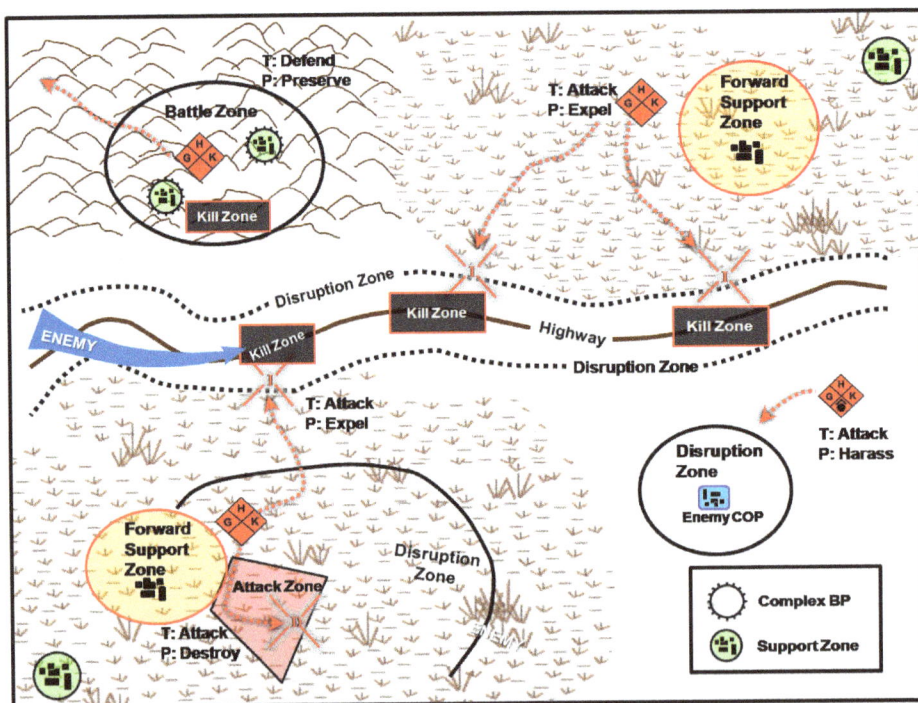

Figure 4-1. GH/K AORs in the Offense.

4-9. Areas of Responsibility.

GH/K Areas of Responsibility (AOR) consist of three basic zones within the Guerrilla Hunter Killer Zone of Operations (Chapter 3): the disruption zone, the battle zone, and the forward support zone. These zones have the same basic purposes in all types of offense. In the offense, the three basic zones may also contain one or more attack zones or kill zones. Zones by be linear or nonlinear in nature. See Figure 2-1 for generalized examples of GH/K zones.

4-10. Disruption Zone.

The disruption zone is where the GH/K sets the conditions for successful operations by beginning the attack on the components f the enemy combat system. A successful disruption one operation can create a window of opportunity that is exploitable in the battle zone. In the disruption zone, the GH/K attacks specific components of the enemy's combat system in order to begin the breakdown of the system.

4-11. Battle Zone.

The battle zone is the portion of the AOR where the GH/K expects to conduct decisive operations. Using all components of combat power, the GH/K will engage the enemy and defeat him in this zone. Units operating in the battle zone can have various missions and objectives, depending on the nature of the overall offensive or defensive operation.

4-12. Forward Support Zone.

The support zone is that area of the Zone of Operations designed to be free of significant enemy action and to permit the effective logistical support of forces. Forward Support Zones are Guerrilla Hunter Killer logistics points located in the GH/K Zone of Operations for easier access to necessary supplies, e.g. food, water, armament. These will assist the GH/K as he conducts operations in the battle zone.

4-13. Attack Zone.

An attack zone is given to a subordinate unit with an offensive mission, to delineate clearly where forces will be conducting offensive maneuver. Attack zones are often used to control offensive action by a subordinate unit inside a larger defensive mission.

4-14. Kill Zone.

A kill zone is a designated area on the battlefield where the GH/K plans to destroy a key enemy target, usually by fires. A kill zone may be within the disruption zone of the battle zone. In defensive operations, it could also be in the support zone. An example would be commonly known in today's Counter Insurgency (COIN) terminology would be known as "IED hot spots."

Chapter 5
Guerrilla Hunter Killer Defensive Operations

The Guerrilla Hunter Killer realizes he is faced with a numerically superior and more technologically advanced enemy, therefore most Guerrilla Hunter Killer operations are offensive, not defensive. There is seldom an attempt to seize and defend objectives for any length of time. However the GH/K will conduct defensive missions to preserve offensive combat power in other areas, to protect an important formation or resource, or to deny access to key facilities or geographic areas. The GH/K will use complex and severely restricted terrain to minimize the enemy's strengths and exploit his weakness.

5-1. Purpose of the defense.
Guerrilla Hunter Killer defensive operations[20] are designed to achieve their overall goals through active measures while preserving combat power. The GH/K conducts three general types of defensive operations according to their purpose: to destroy, preserve, or deny.

5-2. Defense to Destroy.
A defense to destroy is designed to eliminate an attacking formation's ability to continue offensive operations while preserving GH/K forces.

5-3. Defense to Preserve.
A defense to preserve is designed to protect key components of the GH/K from destruction by the enemy, and is the most likely type of defensive operation conducted by the GH/K. Any defensive action taken in a defense to preserve will only be as a delaying effort to allow the Guerrilla Hunter Killer to flee from the battlefield. The GH/K will take full advantage of any existing natural obstacles to prevent the enemy from executing a flanking or encirclement maneuver. If natural obstacles are not present, the GH/K may employ man-made obstacles, such as sloping ditches and Improvised Explosive Devices (IED) to ensure withdrawal from the zone. All obstacles both natural and man-made will be employed so that all paths of escape and roads of access remain free of enemy activity[21]. Such a defense may occur-
- To preserve combat power for future operations
- When facing numerically or qualitatively superior enemy forces

5-4. Defense to Deny.
A defense to deny is intended to deny the enemy access to a geographic area or use of facilities that could enhance his combat operations. A defense to deny will only be conducted in complex terrain that will allow the GH/K an advantage over his enemy, and will only be conducted to preserve an area that the GH/K feels must be retained in order to conduct operations. A defense to deny may quickly transition into a defense to preserve.

5-5. Planned Defense.
A planned defense is a defensive operation undertaken when there is sufficient time and knowledge to prepare forces. Severely restricted terrain is also a pre-requisite for a planned defense. For the Guerrilla Hunter Killer to conduct a planned defense there must be a key component of combat power or terrain that the GH/K feels is worth defending.

5-6. Situational Defense.

The Guerrilla Hunter Killer recognizes that the modern battlefield is chaotic and fleeting opportunities to attack and enemy weakness will continually present themselves and just as quickly disappear. Therefore a GH/K will assess the conditions lending to a situational defense and quickly transition from offensive operations into a situational defense and vice versa.

5-7. Areas of Responsibility.

Guerrilla Hunter Killer AORs in the defense normally consist of three principal zones: disruption, battle and forward support. Zones may be linear of nonlinear in nature and allow the GH/K to transition rapidly between linear and nonlinear operations, as well as offense and defense. Attack and kill zones may also be employed in support of the overall defense.

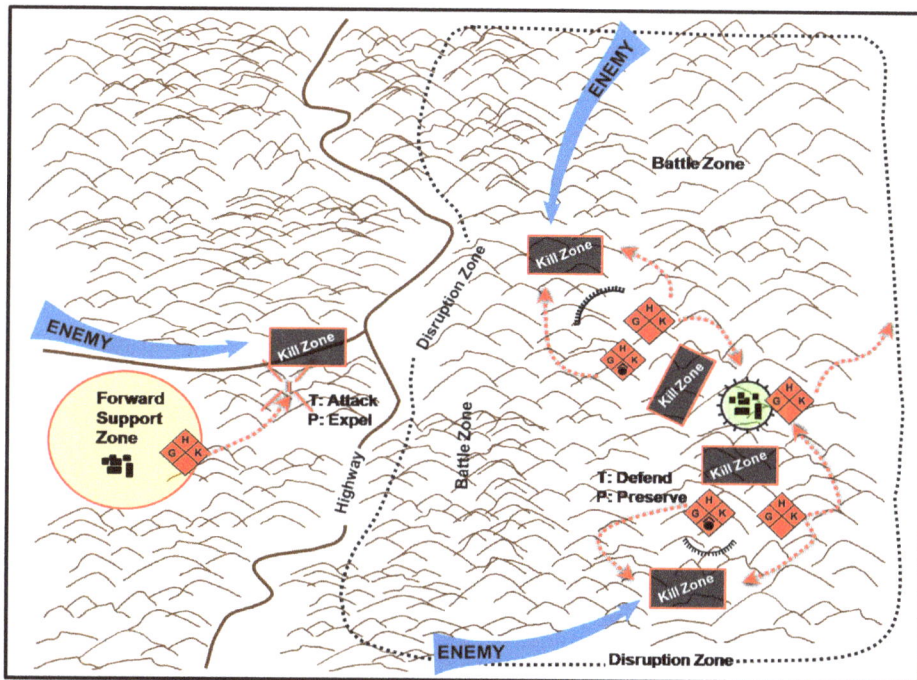

Figure 5-1. GH/K AORs in the Defense.

5-8. Disruption Zone.

In the defense, the disruption zone is that battle space where the Guerrilla Hunter seeks to begin their attack on the designated component or subsystem of the enemy's combat system. The disruption zone is the primary area in which the GH/K commander will employ long range fires. Kill zones can be integrated into the disruption zone.

5-9. Battle Zone.
The battle zone is that battle space in which the GH/K will use fire and maneuver on the enemy force. The battle zone will take full advantage of complex terrain. Kill zones can also be integrated into the battle zone.

5-10. Forward Support Zone.
The support zone is that area of the battle space designed to be free of significant enemy action and to permit the effective logistical support of forces. Forward Support Zones are Guerrilla Hunter Killer logistics points located in the GH/K Zone of Operations for easier access to necessary supplies, e.g. food, water, armament. These will assist the GH/K as he conducts operations in the battle zone.

5-11. Attack Zone.
During an overall defensive operation, and attack zone may be employed to conduct an offensive action inside of a larger defensive action.

5-12. Kill Zone.
A kill zone is a designated area on the battlefield where the Guerrilla Hunter Killer plans to destroy a key enemy target, usually by a standoff weapon such as an Improvised Explosive Device (IED) or a more conventional indirect fire system.

5-13. Battle Position.
The Guerrilla Hunter Killer battle position is a defensive location designed to maximize their ability to accomplish the mission. A battle position is selected such that the terrain in and around it is complementary to the GH/K capabilities and its tactical task. There are two kinds of battle positions: simple and complex.

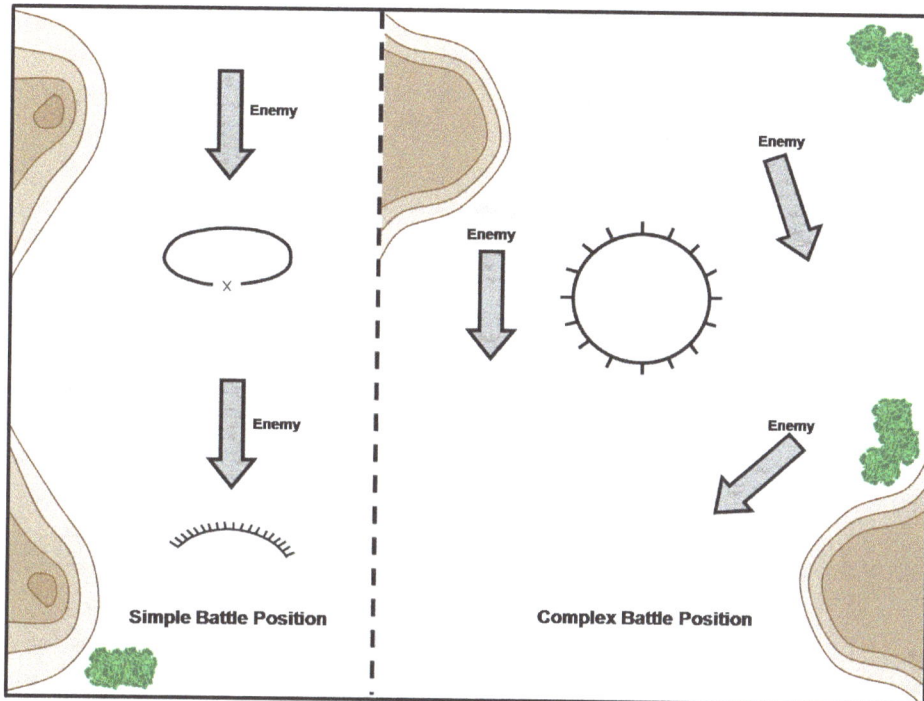

Figure 5-2. Battle Positions.

5-14. Simple Battle Position.

A simple battle position is a defensive location oriented on the most likely enemy avenue of ap-proach. Simple battle positions are not necessarily tied to complex terrain.

5-15. Complex Battle Position.

Complex battle positions are defensive locations designed to protect the GH/K from detection and attack. They typically employ a combination of complex terrain and engineer effort to protect from engagement by precision standoff attack.

This page intentionally left blank.

Chapter 6
Conditions Based Model of Needs

It is important to note the difference between the Maslow Hierarchy model (Figure 6-1a) and the Conditions Based Model of Needs (Figure 6-1b) created to describe the needs as observed in Afghanistan. There are specific and not at all subtle differences between the two, yet the breakdown of the needs that exist have to be measured in accordance with the Host Nation's consideration of those needs. As in Maslow's model, the fact that each lower tier has to be completely satisfied holds true to the model developed by the 5/2 ID (SBCT) ACE. Below are graphics showing the comparison of the hierarchal needs:

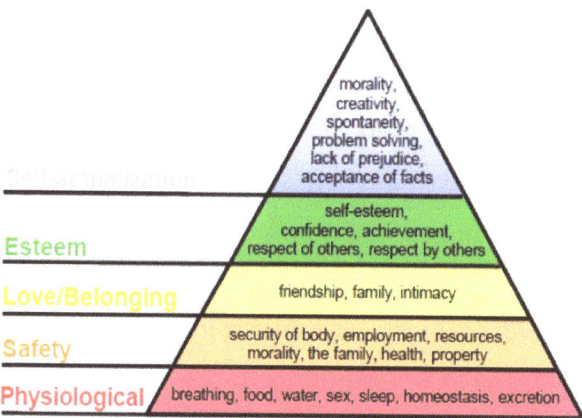

Figure 6-1a. MASLOW'S HIERARCHY OF NEEDS   Figure 6-1b. CONDITIONS BASED HIERARCHY

Most important to note is the Fluidity of Neutrality as seen in model developed by the 5/2 ID (SBCT) ACE.

The Fluidity of Neutrality can be defined as the continual change of physical and social conditions placed upon an individual that causes shifts in the perceptions of the individual's determined need at any given time.

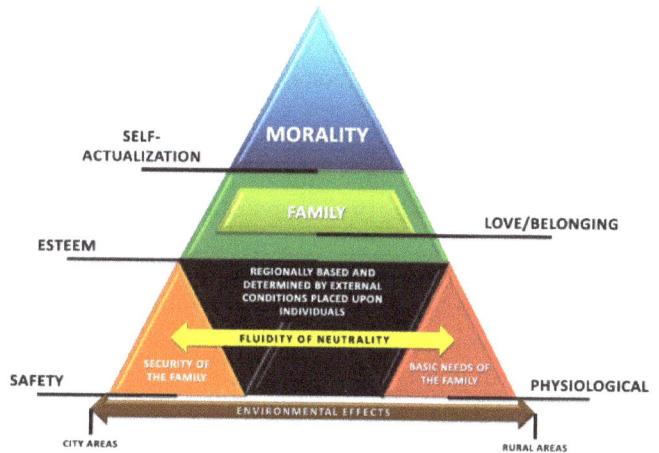

The Conditions Based Hierarchy differs from Maslow's Hierarchy of Needs in that the tiers of Safety and Physiological needs are adjacent to each other. The aspects of the Environmental Effects of the terrain between the more populated City Areas and the less populated Rural Areas are represented as the most constant and identifiable settings where conditions initiate shifts in the ability for needs at this tier to be fulfilled. The additional sets of conditions which cause shifts in the Fluidity of Neutrality are primarily social based events. With the City and Rural areas still used as constants, the social based events become the identifiable set of conditions which shifts the Fluidity of Neutrality. These social based conditions are initiated through the actions, or lack thereof, by either the External Military Advisers or the Guerrilla Forces. Given the immense ground area of Afghanistan, the constants of the City or Rural areas outline identifiable locations where External Military Advisers and Guerrilla Forces efforts are or are not present. This zoning of effort identifies the areas where the needs of the people are more or less likely to be influenced by ones adversary.

The Fluidity of Neutrality has to be consistently monitored in order to identify when the needs of the populace are and are not being met. Without addressing this lower tier, progression to the higher tiers is difficult to achieve. The efforts of External Military Advisers and Civil Aid Organizations are needed to enable the Host Nation's ability to aid the local populace's fulfillment of higher needs. The lack of an applied effort from the External Military Advisors and Civil Aid Organizations prevents the Host Nation Government from achieving acceptance by the populace. That being said, the Host Nation Government has to be able to provide the requirements needed to continually win support from the populace which begins with the sense of accomplishment of the lower physiological and safety needs amongst the populace.

If these needs are unmonitored and left unfulfilled, Guerrilla forces quickly identify the void as a vulnerability and immediately capitalize upon the gap, thus enabling the efforts of the Guerrillas to be accepted by the local populace. Once the Guerrilla effort has been accepted by the populace, Guerrilla Forces further develop the Base Camp Zone and instill an Internal Civil Organization (oftentimes referred to as the Shadow Government) which continually works to reduce, if not, neutralize the established Host Nation Government's presence or influence within the zone. The efforts of the Guerrilla forces are enacted as being either responsive to or exploitative of the needs of the local populace.

Being that the enemy is indigenous to the region, identifying how Guerrilla forces perceive the needs of the social environment across the terrain best outlines the anticipated effects the enemy hopes to achieve across the human terrain. Both Needs Models depict the Safety and Physiological needs as the foundation by which all other needs are built upon. However, the Fluidity of Neutrality incorporated into the model developed by 5/2 ID (SBCT) ACE identifies how the actions of both the Host Nation Government and Guerrilla forces are social factors across the environment acting as the impetus which shifts the weight of consideration amongst the local populace as to who best supports the fulfillment of their Physiological and Safety needs.

COMPARING THE MODELS

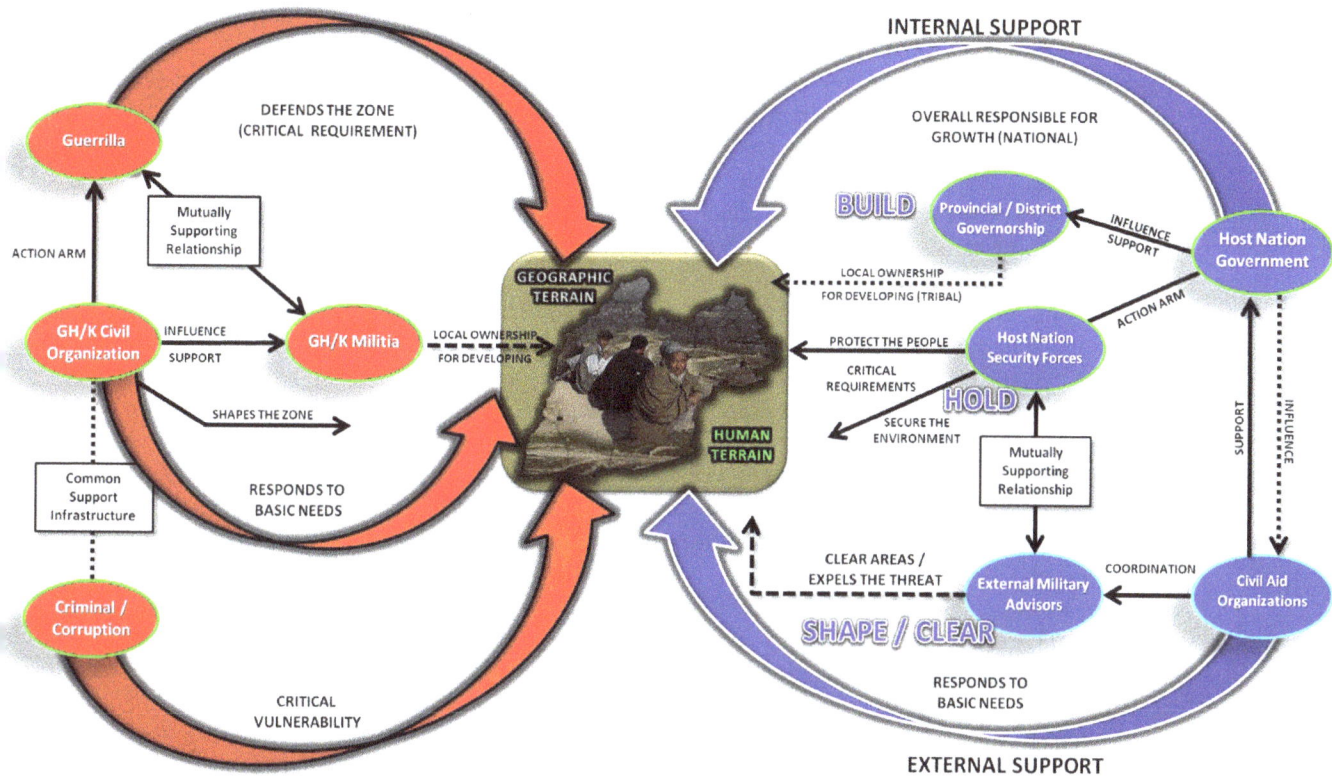

Figure 7-1. Comparison of the GH/K and the Host Nation Operational Models

7-1. The Guerrilla Hunter Killer And The Host Nation Government.

The Operational Model (Figure 1) breaks down the Host Nation Government vs. GH/K views by opposing sides. Observing the model becomes convoluted unless the relationship between these two opposing sides, are well understood.

The objective is control, making the central representation of Human Terrain and Geographic Terrain critical requirements for the Host Nation Government and GH/K Forces to switch support in favor of one side or the other.

The needs around the center represent two basic areas of concern: Human and Geographical terrain. Inside of both models, the contingency most afflicted as prescribed by COIN is the human terrain with a large focus on human needs. The GH/K focuses on this aspect as well by paying particular attention to the geographic terrain and controlling that prior to controlling the human terrain. By controlling the geographic terrain, the GH/K is able to supply, on call, necessities of life that usurp control of the human terrain from the efforts of the Host Nation Government.

Chapter 7

Zones of Operations to suppress the Host Nation Forces in that zone.

When monitoring terrain, both human and geographic, and needs across those opposing factors, the human terrain is only a small factor. The structure of the needs across the two separate terrains cannot be made stable until both sides are equally satisfied. By closely structuring operations around only one terrain, human or physical, the other will not stay stable. One issue with paying too close attention to one or the other is the ease by which the scale tips away from the favor of the Host Nation Government's intent.

Geographic needs should not be measured only by land ownership, but by area of influence to where human needs can be marked by spheres of influence. Concentration inside of those spheres of influence eliminates the geographic terrain consideration because geographic terrain does not affect the human in the same manner as simple needs. In other words, physical terrain does not necessarily have an impact on the human needs. Separately, given that physical terrain does not affect the human needs the same in every area, it is logical to find that the security of terrain does directly affect the human. Operations that exclude securing the terrain (zone) by not allocating enough forces to appropriately secure the zone is an operational consideration that ultimately loses the human needs to the adversary. The effort of the Guerrilla forces is to manage the balancing act of securing the terrain (zone) to promote success across the human terrain.

GH/K Forces deliver a model of security, albeit one that may not be widely accepted by the populace, but is every bit as important. They offer this model of security in terrain and not through the most populated areas as centers of gravity, which allows the GH/K control over the rural areas, thus allowing for larger pockets of support where supply can easily take place. With GH/K operations focusing more on securing more areas of open and rural terrain, they are free to move around the population centers of gravity where they are contested, into other geographic areas that they are not contested. The limited contact in the denser population is used to develop their

Once the GH/K is in control of the zone, they are able to move into other areas and continue with the same model of focusing on security of the terrain as opposed to human needs alone. One might argue that human needs, to a large scale, then becomes part of the geographic needs and therefore tips the scale to the side of the GH/K effort. Ultimately by controlling the geographic terrain, the guerilla has developed more area under their control, which causes shifts in perceptions eventually creating a preconceived notion that the legitimate (Host Nation) government does not have any interest or effort in the area (Zone), this locally translates to a determination that there isn't any concern for the people in the area.

The Guerrilla Hunter Killer Operational Model
As Applied to the Conditions Based Hierarchy

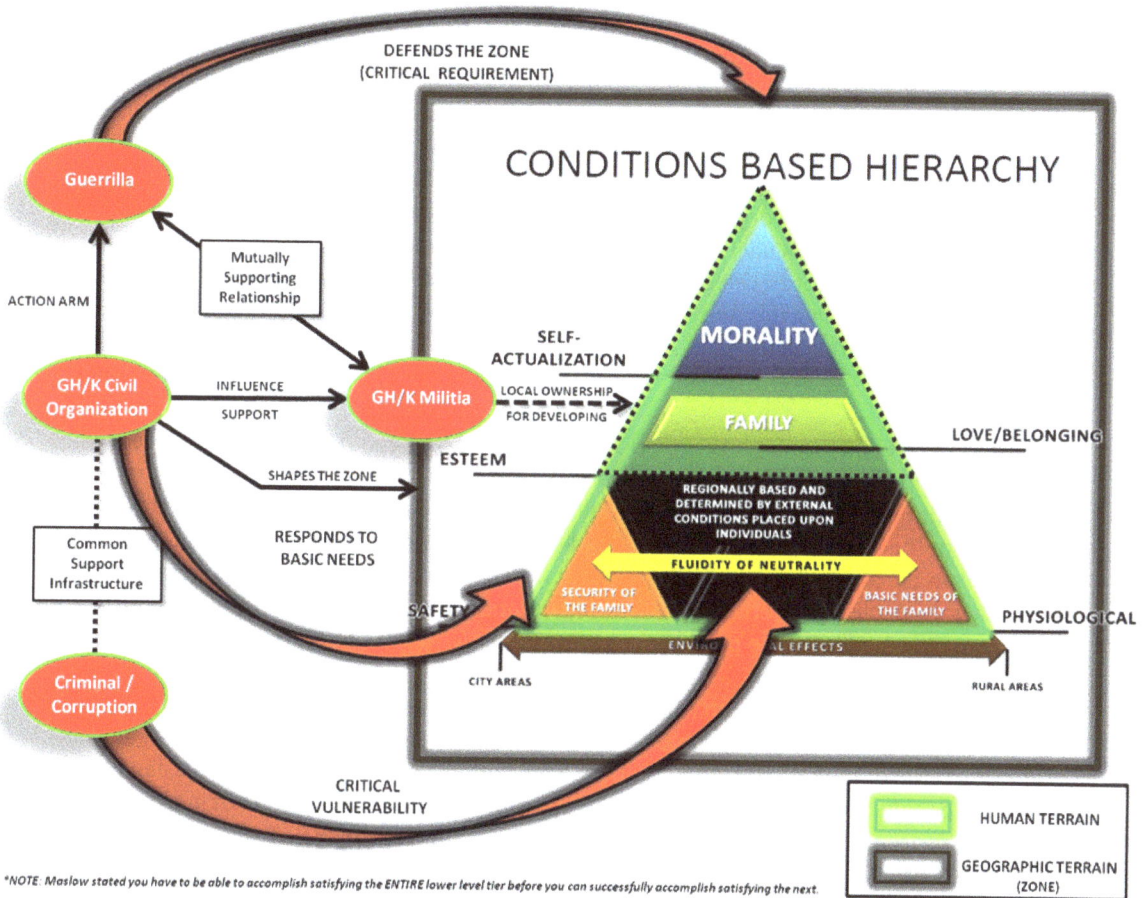

Figure 8-1. Guerrilla Hunter Killer Operational Model.

The Guerrilla Hunter Killer Operational Model uses the Conditions Based Model of Needs to conceptualize the efforts applied by each element of the GH/K formation in regards to the Human Terrain (Needs of the Populace) and Physical Terrain (Zones). In needs assessment, the conditions based model accounts for environmental considerations as a constant to identify potential areas (Zones) where there is likely to be a greater Physiological Need amongst the populace. The Host Nation Government, as well as the GH/K forces, know to the best of detail what the basis of needs are and how best to affect them. This local knowledge of zones and needs are complicated by the tribal dynamics of the environment and can potentially create further disenfranchisement amongst the populace if the efforts of external advisors and civil organizations (Coalition Forces), the Host Nation Government, or even the Internal GH/K Civil Organization (IGH/KCO) are perceived as being misaligned due to any form of preferential decision-making based upon tribal affiliations.

Chapter 8

The shifting in the Fluidity of Neutrality identifies that no single need is more important than any other across the environment. The requirements of needs are first used to determine the zones based upon what environment effects are likely causing a higher physiological need. Therefore, when the neutrality fails from one side to the other; the basic needs are not met.

GH/K efforts focus on this Critical Vulnerability because it is the easiest to affect and also the hardest for the Host Nation Government to defend. The establishment of an Internal GH/K Civil Organization (IGH/KCO) to respond and support the needs at this level usurps the best effort of the external advisors and civil organization as the zone is under the control of the GH/K forces. This form of an Internal GH/K Civil Organization (IGH/KCO) as a Shadow Governance can best be described as the portions of any illegitimate governorship needed to establish a local level perception of legitimacy. Using this, the Internal GH/K Civil Organization (IGH/KCO) governance immediately responds to the needs across the zone and rebuilds the area under their chosen set and form of laws.

Once the Internal GH/K Civil Organization (IGH/KCO) is established in zone, the GH/K Forces recruit people indigenous to the area as the local Militia to shape the support zones and as representatives from the local populace. This employment of the GH/K Militia directly ties the responsibility for the next tier of needs in the Conditions Based Model of Needs to those local members from the area. The militia is the basis of the shaping effort in the human terrain so that the newly established Internal GH/K Civil Organization (IGH/KCO) achieves stability as a locally form of governance for the people.

The Internal GH/K Civil Organization (IGH/KCO), or Shadow Governance, assists with higher needs as required because the ties the GH/K Militia have to the people are set along the Familial portion of the Needs model. The GH/K Militia are presented as defenders of the basic needs in favor of the people. These familial relationships are easier to influence and do not necessarily require additional assistance from the Internal GH/K Civil Organization (IGH/KCO). That being said, the GH/K Militia, being of the people, will typically become a policing effort once there is more acceptance of the Internal GH/K Civil Organization (IGH/KCO) by the extended family members of the GH/K Militia across the zone.

The GH/K forces are explicitly responsible for the security of all the identified and established zones. The objective of these forces is to diminish the focus of the Host Nation Government and any External Military Advisers long enough for the Internal GH/K Civil Organization (IGH/KCO) and GH/K Militia to develop, shape, and ultimately bring the local populace in the zone to accept and/or tolerate their presence. Once this has been achieved, the GH/K has accomplished control over the zone and begins its efforts to expand the zone as needed.

Chapter 9
The Host Nation Operational Model
As Applied To Maslow's Hierarchy of Needs

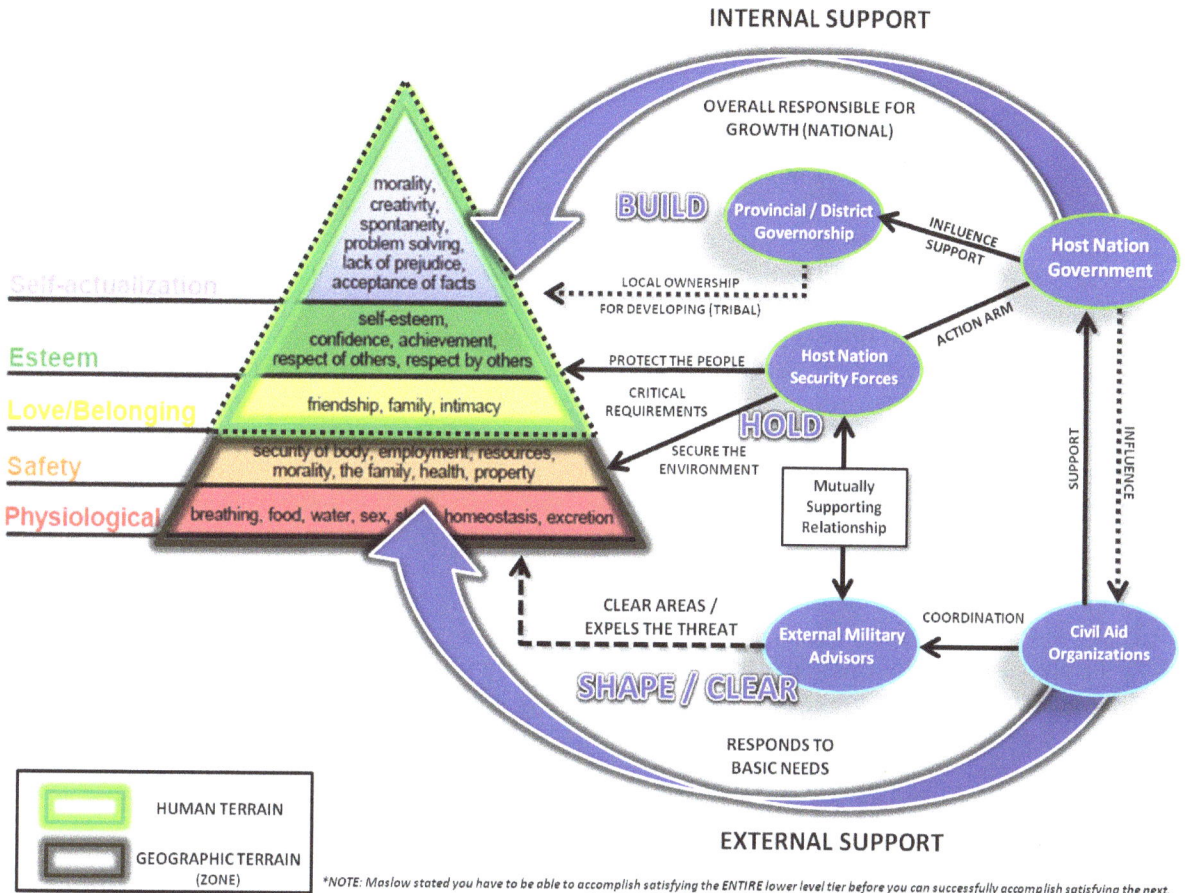

INTERNAL SUPPORT

OVERALL RESPONSIBLE FOR
GROWTH (NATIONAL)

BUILD

Provincial / District
Governorship

INFLUENCE
SUPPORT

Host Nation
Government

morality,
creativity,
spontaneity,
problem solving,
lack of prejudice,
acceptance of facts

Self-actualization

LOCAL OWNERSHIP
FOR DEVELOPING (TRIBAL)

ACTION ARM

self-esteem,
confidence, achievement,
respect of others, respect by others

PROTECT THE PEOPLE

Host Nation
Security Forces

Esteem

Love/Belonging

friendship, family, intimacy

CRITICAL
REQUIREMENTS

HOLD

SUPPORT

INFLUENCE

Safety

security of body, employment, resources,
morality, the family, health, property

SECURE THE
ENVIRONMENT

Mutually
Supporting
Relationship

Physiological

breathing, food, water, sex, sleep, homeostasis, excretion

CLEAR AREAS /
EXPELS THE THREAT

COORDINATION

External Military
Advisors

Civil Aid
Organizations

SHAPE / CLEAR

RESPONDS TO
BASIC NEEDS

HUMAN TERRAIN

GEOGRAPHIC TERRAIN
(ZONE)

EXTERNAL SUPPORT

*NOTE: Maslow stated you have to be able to accomplish satisfying the ENTIRE lower level tier before you can successfully accomplish satisfying the next.

Figure 9-1. The Host Nation Operational Model.

When dealing with the needs assessment, the only thing to be considered as constant between *Maslow's Hierarchy of Needs* model and *Conditions Based Model of Needs* is that the next level of needs cannot be satisfied until the prior level are completely satisfied. In the Host Nation Government's Operational Model (centered on Maslow's model) the Civil Aid Organization and the External Military Advisors develop the basic lower two levels of needs.

After the efforts of the External Support have cleared the geographic terrain from of the Guerrilla forces, the Host Nation Security Forces become the leading organization responsible for securing the geographic terrain. This effort by the Host Nation Security Forces is a critical requirement for control of the zone to continue for the Host Nation Government's growth through the Provincial and District level leadership.

26 July 2009   GUERRILLA HUNTER KILLER SMARTBOOK   9-1

The External Military Advisors have a continual effort applied to supporting the Host Nation Security Force, but as the External Military Advisers move to other geographic areas to clear the GH/K Forces. The departed area being managed by the efforts of the Host Nation Security Forces become unstable. GH/K Forces work to degrade safety, and ensure that all needs cannot be met so that no matter how secure the perceived environment is security can never be entirely achieved.

The Host Nation Operational Model (Figure 1) depicts that the External Military Advisers and Civil Aid Organizations succeed during their operations across the geographic terrain. However, the exchange of responsibility for the Geographic Terrain from the External Military Advisers to the Host Nation Security Forces and Provincial/District Governorship to manage both the Geographic Terrain along with the Human Terrain creates instability and challenges the Host Nation Government's overall effort. As this model is applied across multiple areas, the resultant effect is a fluctuation of stability across broader areas which has a greater affect of the human terrain and depreciates any formed confidence that the efforts of the Host Nation Government has had on the people.

External GH/K Civil Organizations will use physical intimidation, assassination, and criminal activity to disrupt the populated areas which are the centers of gravity for the environment. Therefore, safety will not be determined adequate enough for the Host Nation Government to raise public esteem or confidence in those areas for taking ownership of the nation.

Part of the goal of the External Military Advisors is to develop the Host Nation Security Forces to enable them to secure the environment. As displayed in the Host Nation Operational Model, the Civil Aid Organization, the External Military Advisors, and the Host Nation Security Forces have to achieve satisfaction of the physiological and safety needs prior to the Host Nation governmental effort at the Provincial and District level to rebuild and progress the higher needs amongst the populace by fully securing zones. It is a critical requirement for the Host Nation Government, through the Host Nation Security Forces to clear, secure, and control zones above and beyond that of the GH/K forces to raise the majority of the populace above the base level needs of Safety and Physiological concerns.

Chapter 10
The Guerrilla Hunter Killer Operational Cycle

10-1. The Cycle of Phases.

GH/K Forces use the Zone of Operations to lessen the Host Nation effort to the population centers of as the center of gravity. In doing so, they cause the Host Nation to claim success in the few areas under their control which are the most developed, but least important to sustaining the GH/K effort. This reduction of the center of gravity in turn also disables the ability for the Host Nation to achieve security in the more remote and less popular or populated areas. With a high focus of the Host Nation on securing the population centers of gravity, the GH/K forces are then more easily able to develop other zones: Zones of Security and Base Camp Zones.

In the Zones of Security, the GH/K Force trains, mentors, and utilizes local militants to conduct disruptive activity in order to degrade the Host Nation's success in zone and at the same time, set the conditions to develop a Base Camp Zone. Once the conditions have been set, the GH/K Forces begin to establish the Internal GH/K Civil Organization to provide their form of legitimate governance. The local militants, becoming proficient in their training, progress from the status of militia and are developed into independently functioning GH/K Teams with directed responsibilities. GH/K Forces continue this cycle to restart the process of developing conditions in another Zone of Security to develop other Base Camp Zones. This method is used to quickly multiply the force and establish the same cycle across the region.

Once the Base Camp Zone is established, the focus turns inwards to the development of the Internal GH/K Civil Organization, or Shadow Government, to develop a legitimate government inside of the Base Camp Zone. Once done, the GH/K Force uses external enablers to begin the process back into the Zone of Security. GH/K Contacts are again made with elements of the populace that are receptive to the GH/K presence. The GH/K Militia will be redeveloped until another Base Camp Zone is developed.

The goal of the GH/K Force is to reduce the size of their operating zone, thus, increasing the Zone of Security. This portion is particularly important because the Base Camp Zone cycle cannot be started in the Zone of Operations because of heavy presence of the Host Nation Security Forces and External Military Advisors.

By decreasing their Zone of Operations, the GH/K Forces effectively limit the amount of contact that the Host Nation has with more of the populace within the zone under control by the Internal GH/K Civil Organization. Once the GH/K have successfully pushed forward the limits of the Zone of Security (possibly considered the Forward Line of Enemy Troops) the terrain, both human and physical, are reassessed as to which areas will be plausible to derive the most disruption with the GH/K Forces across each zone.

The ultimate goal, again, is to increase the Zone of Security, limit the Zone of Operations, and set the overall conditions to establish a Base Camp Zones where the GH/K Force will have success in developing a legitimate Internal GH/K Civil Organization presence to carry out the functions of providing Medical, Judicial (Courts), Facilitation, IED Production, and Training for GH/K Forces in the greater area.

The establishment of zones by GH/K Forces are arranged through a cycle of phases (figure 1). The process begins in a populated area and cycles through the human terrain to establish Base Camp Zones. After a Base Camp Zone is established, the cycle starts again. The next section outlines the typical efforts that progress by phase during the GH/K Cycle.

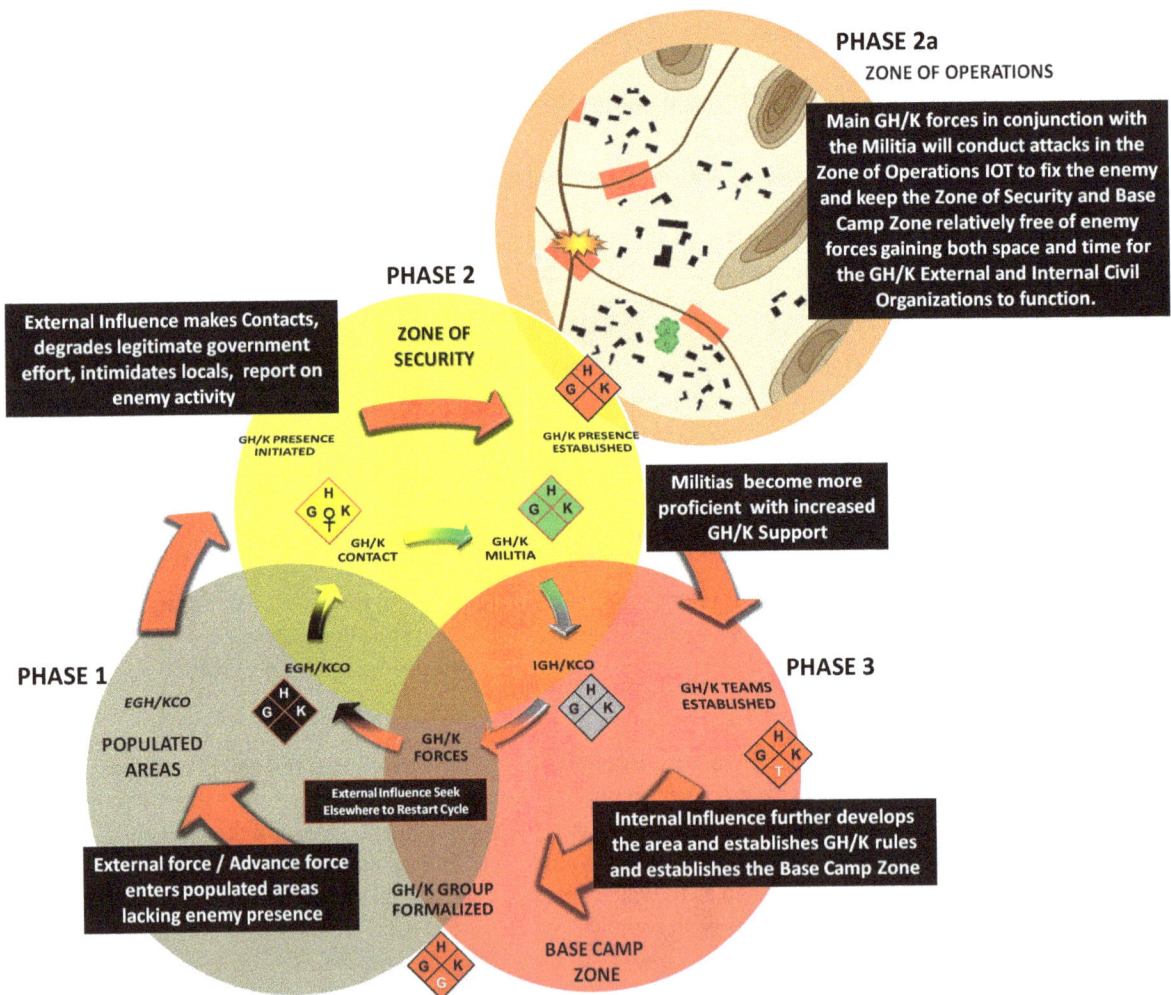

Figure 10-1. The Cycle of Phases.

10-2. Phase 1: Populated Areas initiate the creation of Zones.
- External GH/K Civil Organization achieves makes GH/K Contacts through denied or disenfranchised portions of the population
- External GH/K Civil Organization and GH/K Contacts identify, adopt (recruit), and train members of the local Population into the GH/K Militia and well trained GH/K Force
- External GH/K Civil Organizations carry out their main tasks to degrade security in populated city areas and initiate assassinations, kidnapping, and intimidation campaigns.

10-3. Phase 2: GH/K Zone of Security.
- GH/K Contacts and GH/K Militia fully integrate themselves within the areas of the local population of the zone
- By training, mentoring, and supplying local militia
- By using GH/K and militia to establish Support Zones and GH/K Camps in and around the area
- Set conditions to expand Zone of Security
- Use well trained GH/K Teams to protect and shape areas of Zone of Security primed to develop Base Camp Zone

10-4. Phase 2a: GH/K Zone of Operations.
- GH/K Teams and GH/K Militia identify areas within the Zone of Security as Disruption Zones.
- GH/K Forces create an Early Warning System through the use of the GH/K Militia and GH/K Contacts
- Establishment of Forward Support Zones in the vicinity of Attack Zones to caches weapons
- GH/K Forces identify patterns in the Host Nation and External Military Advisors Operations to determine where the terrain best supports the creation of a Kill Zone.
- The GH/K Forces use the Zone of Operations as a culmination point for their offensive efforts to degrade the Host Nation and External Military Advisors ability to conduct operations through the Zone of Security down into the Base Camp Zones

10-5. Phase 3: GH/K Base Camp Zones.
- GH/K Forces develop Internal GH/K Civil Organization to enact Governance under the define GH/K precepts
- The Internal GH/K Civil Organization employ efforts to assist the population by satisfying needs
- Seek sparsely populated areas that are capable of being used to support the GH/K effort
- Act as distant rear areas for GH/K forces return to after operations into Zone of Operations
- Identifies Zone of Security limits further inside of Zone of Operations
- Establishes Internal GH/K Civil Organization functions to provide Medical, Judicial (Courts), Facilitation, IED Production, and Training for GH/K Forces in the Area
- Location where Command and Control is capable of managing GH/K efforts while still distanced from the major operating areas of the Host Nation and External Military Advisors

This page intentionally left blank.

Chapter 11
Process for Defining the Threat in the DCGS-A MFWS

11-1. Create Threat Template.
The process for designating a GH/K Formation begins with an ACE OB Technician researching reporting to outline a DOCTEMP, as defined by the GH/K Reference Guide.

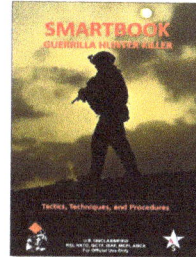

11-2. Query Data Sources.
The Area Fusion Teams continuously search the 58 Message Data Sources that are populated into DCGS-A through the Multifunction Workstation (MFWS) Query Tree Search Application.

11-3. Create Entities.
Area Fusion Teams create and database entities of analytical relevance to support the development of their respective areas of responsibility.

      a. After the Area Fusion Teams database Entities, Links are created to accurately account for the relationships which exist between entities in the dataset based upon how information in the reports are actually outlined.

11-4. Review Template against the Entities in the Threat Entities Database (TED) .
After Entities have been created in the database, linked, and saved to the TED, the Area Fusion Teams review the current GH/K Formation Template for their area and identify Entities that are related to the GH/K Formation.

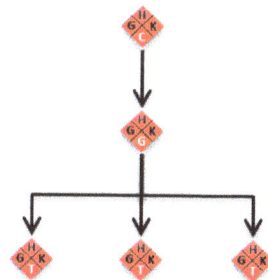

11-5. Link Entities to Threat Formations.

The Area Fusion Teams begin linking relationships between people, events, locations, or other factors deemed significant to the GH/K Formation. The linking of Entities to the GH/K Formation is done as needed based upon an Analysts determination that the associated reporting for an entity supports the Link Relationship to the GH/K Formation.

11-6. Update Threat Formations.

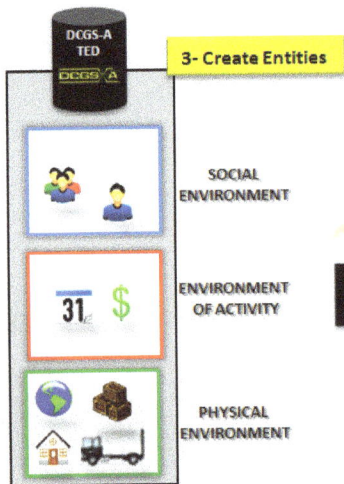

While the GH/K Formation Template is being linked to and updated with Entities by the Area Fusion Teams , the ACE OB Technician reviews the new relationships that have been added to reconfirm and validate the GH/K Formation based upon the Entities, reporting for the given area, and the GH/K Zones overview.

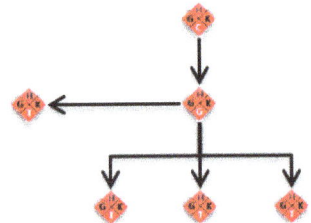

2- Query Data Sources

1- Create Threat Template

6- Update Threat Formations

As the Threat Formations are updated they move to become the SITTEMP that Analysts use to Define the Current Threat Picture

3- Create Entities

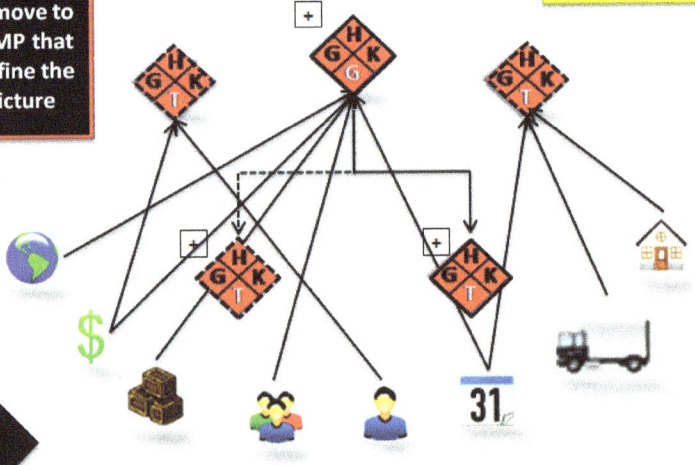

SOCIAL ENVIRONMENT

ENVIRONMENT OF ACTIVITY

PHYSICAL ENVIRONMENT

4- Review Template against the TED Entities

5- Link Entities to Threat Formations *(as needed)*

Process Overview

Chapter 12
Databases

Databases provide systematic processing and automated parsing, using intelligence operations standardized forms, into appropriate databases for information storing, sharing, retrieval, and analysis allow query functions for decision-making, as well as operational and analytical support. And provide analytical programs able to correlate data that facilitate information retrieval from any data repository. They Incorporate information retrieval functions, such as browsing, Boolean functions, key word searching, concept searches, and similar functions

12-1.Environments.
An all source intelligence database is comprised of information from three areas across the data source repositories:
- Physical Environment
- Social Environment
- Environment of Activity (Events)

12-2. Functions.
Without databases, ***information is difficult, or impossible to retrieve quickly***, especially under adverse conditions. Databases support many complex analytical functions and requirements, to Include:
- Threat and friendly situations tracking
- Summary, report, and assessment preparation
- Targeting
- RFIs
- Mission Deconfliction

This is what the Multi-Function Workstation (MFWS) provides

12-3. Analysis.
Databases that interact with other tools to ***support predictive analysis, prepare graphic analytical products, and provide situational awareness, down to unit commanders***. These databases:
- Support time event charts
- Association matrixes
- Link analysis,
- Other analytical tools

Chapter 13
Entity Environments

The nine (9) entity types within the MFWS are the building blocks for data basing information.

13-1. Entity Types.
The Entity Types are easily categorized to represent the Physical, Social, and activity environments. The available entity types are:

- Equipment
- Vehicle
- Event
- Facility
- Organization
- Person
- Financial Transaction
- Place

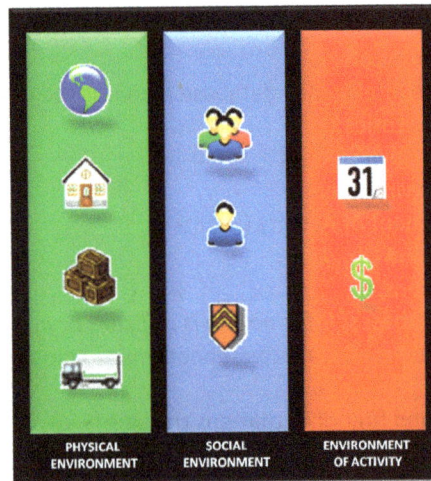

13-2. Entity Categories.
The categorization of each entity into an environment forms the structure of the database once it is brought together in the TED.

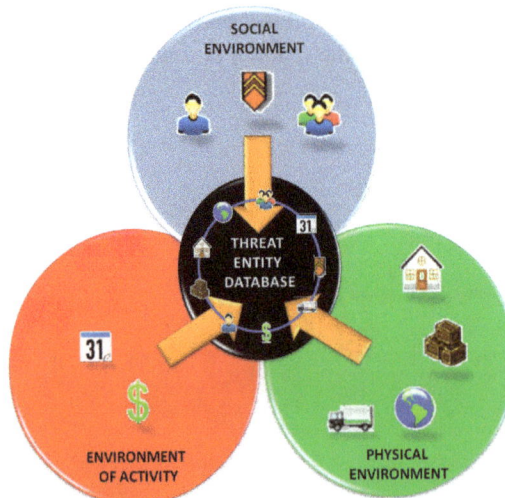

Chapter 14
Entity Properties Standards

Standardizing the entity database begins with a reduction in the total number of Entity Property Fields. By doing this it will allow the BDE ACE to best capture the most relevant information during the Analysts processing of reporting.

14-1. Property Fields.
Across all Entity Types the less relevant Property Fields have been hidden on the system to reduce the number of fields that an Analyst will have to work with.

*** NOTE: This is a system configuration change and will have to be done either automatically during a reimage of each BAL or manually under the Settings Option.**

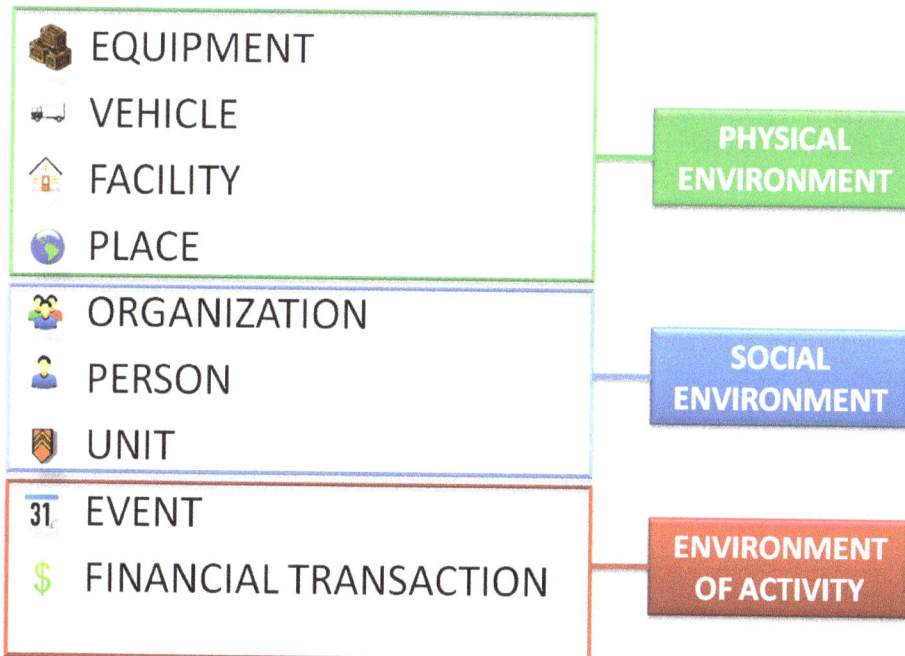

EQUIPMENT

VEHICLE

FACILITY

PLACE

PHYSICAL ENVIRONMENT

ORGANIZATION

PERSON

UNIT

SOCIAL ENVIRONMENT

31. EVENT

$ FINANCIAL TRANSACTION

ENVIRONMENT OF ACTIVITY

Chapter 15
Integrated Intelligence Functions within 5/2 ID SBCT Operations in Afghanistan

This Smartbook was written to provide company through brigade level operators a reference for 5/2 ID SBCT MFWS data standards. This manual also contains information on utilizing the DCGS Integrated Backbone (DIB) which expands database searches to resources outside of DCGS-A MFWS itself.

15-1. Making Intelligence History in Afghanistan.

Intelligence analysts under 5/2 ID SBCT are in a position to made intelligence history. Never before has US Army intelligence at the company to brigade level been able to integrate intelligence information as quickly and seamlessly as can be done with 5/2 ID SBCT's implementation of the Distributed Common Ground System (DCGS). DCGS use in 5/2 ID SBCT area of operations was more robust, and tightly integrated into command operations than in any other sector in Afghanistan.

15-2. Why is Full Integration Important?

5/2 ID SBCT fought an amorphous enemy, whose operators and suppliers moved discretely across the battle space, blending into civilian populations when possible to avoid detection.

As intelligence personnel providing timely, accurate, and relevant intelligence to support the commanders decision making process, we were tasked with building the 'big picture' of enemy operations, so that our commanders could plan appropriate operations. 21st century sensor technology and Human Intelligence (HUMINT) professionals aid us in detecting the enemy, but the complete picture of enemy operations and intentions can only be created by fusing reporting from all intelligence sources at all levels.

15-3. Central Information Repository for All to Utilize.

In past conflicts, the central repository of intelligence information existed at the higher echelons of command, and lower echelon users had to request information from adjacent or higher command to build 'big picture' intelligence estimates. By using the DCGS– A MFWS analysts at all levels have access to information unimpeded by request processes to other units.

15-4. Garbage In, Garbage Out.

It is important to understand that normalization of data is key to success in shared databases. Entities must be uniformly marked within the database so users can locate all related information on a particular person, organization, object, or event.

a. As the intelligence data is extracted during DCGS-A operations, information going into the Tactical Entity Database (TED) must be reviewed for accuracy or format after operator entry. It is therefore crucial that analysts operating the DCGS-A MFWS understand and abide to a prescribed data entry standard.

Chapter 16
MFWS Entity Standards

This section contains information how to configure the DCGS-A MFWS per the 5/2 ID SBCT ACE recommendations for data entry standards into the MFWS Tactical Entity Database (TED) .

16-1. MFWS System Field Configuration.
Configuring MFWS for data entry is a two step process. Field visibility for each entity type must be set in System Preferences; then again the matching fields must be switched on in Quickforms Setup.

a. Select System from the dropdown menu.

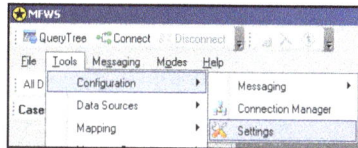

b. Choose each entity type using the lower dropdown menu (Event entity shown).

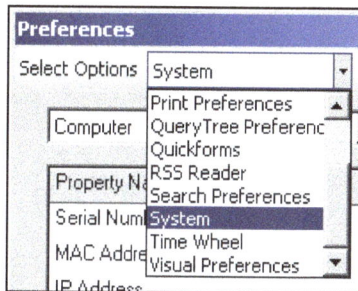

c. Adjust 'visible' field to follow Appendix 1 for each entity type.

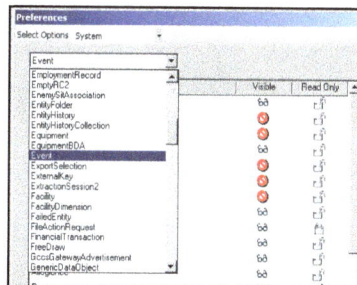

Chapter 16

16-2. Check fields in QuickForms Setup.

In this step, you essentially repeat the process, using check boxes to activate/deactivate fields in Quickforms.

a. Open Quickforms Setup using this menu path; Tools >> Configuration >> Settings >> Quickforms (from dropdown menu).

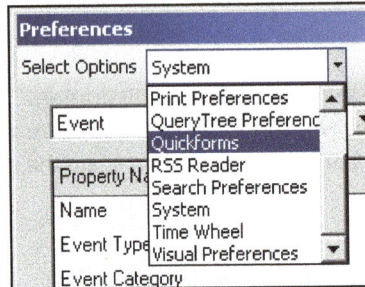

b. Check darkened boxes under 'QuickFormsRequired'.

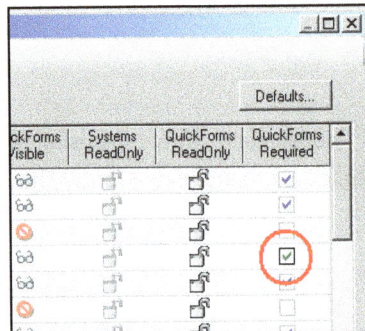

Chapter 17
MFWS Data Entry Formatting

Equipment Entity

PROPERTY FIELD	STANDARD
NAME	ALL CAPS WITH (( )) FOR ASSOC REF*
LOCATIONS	ADD GEO LOCATION DATA TO THE LOCATIONS TAB
DATE FIRST INFO	DATE OF INFO FROM REPORT, USE THE CALENDAR TO SELECT DATE
DATE LAST MODIFIED	AUTOMATICALLY FILLED IN
SYMBOL CODE	AUTOMATICALLY FILLED IN
AFFILIATION	DROP DOWN SELECTION FOR AFFILIATION
ALLEGIANCE	DROP DOWN SELECTION FOR COUNTRY
COUNTRY	DROP DOWN SELECTION FOR COUNTRY
OPERATIONAL STATUS	DROP DOWN SELECTION FOR STATUS
INTELLIGENCE EVALUATION	DROP DOWN SELECTION FOR EVALUATION
SECURITY INFO	AUTOMATICALLY FILLED IN

Vehicle Entity

PROPERTY FIELD	STANDARD
NAME	ALL CAPS WITH (( )) FOR ASSOC REF*
LOCATIONS	ADD GEO LOCATION DATA TO THE LOCATIONS TAB
DATE FIRST INFO	DATE OF INFO FROM REPORT, USE THE CALENDAR TO SELECT DATE
DATE LAST MODIFIED	AUTOMATICALLY FILLED IN
SYMBOL CODE	AUTOMATICALLY FILLED IN
AFFILIATION	DROP DOWN SELECTION FOR AFFILIATION
ALLEGIANCE	DROP DOWN SELECTION FOR COUNTRY
COUNTRY	DROP DOWN SELECTION FOR COUNTRY
YEAR	FREETEXT FIELD: NUMBERS ONLY; NO ABBREVIATIONS

FERTILIZER ((DAMAN))
(DCGSIOP-KAF9:TED)

Name	FERTILIZER ((DAMAN))
Locations	41RQR5404311367
Date First Info	29 0300Z Nov 2009
Date Last Modified	30 1958Z Nov 2009
Symbol Code	SUGPE----*"AF"
Affiliation	Inconclusive Analysis
Allegiance	AFGHANISTAN
Country	AFGHANISTAN
Operational Status	Ready, 5 - Not Immediately
Intelligence Evaluation	Confirmed

DELIVERY VEHICLE ((SHA JOY))
(DCGSIOP-KAF9:TED)

Name	DELIVERY VEHICLE ((SHA JOY))
Locations	41SPR9168067950
Date First Info	29 0600Z Nov 2009
Date Last Modified	30 1313Z Nov 2009
Symbol Code	SUGPEV----*"AF"
Affiliation	Inconclusive Analysis
Allegiance	AFGHANISTAN
Country	AFGHANISTAN
Year	2003

Chapter 17

Facility Entity

PROPERTY FIELD	STANDARD
NAME	ALL CAPS WITH (( )) FOR ASSOC REF*
LOCATIONS	ADD GEO LOCATION DATA TO THE LOCATIONS TAB
DATE FIRST INFO	DATE OF INFO FROM RE-PORT, USE THE CALENDAR TO SELECT DATE
DATE LAST MODIFIED	AUTOMATICALLY FILLED IN
SYMBOL CODE	AUTOMATICALLY FILLED IN
AFFILIATION	DROP DOWN SELECTION FOR AFFILIATION
ALLEGIANCE	DROP DOWN SELECTION FOR COUNTRY
COUNTRY	DROP DOWN SELECTION FOR COUNTRY
INTELLIGENCE EVALUATION	DROP DOWN SELECTION FOR CONDITION
CONDITION	DROP DOWN SELECTION FOR CONDITION
SECURITY INFO	AUTOMATICALLY FILLED IN

Place Entity

PROPERTY FIELD	STANDARD
NAME	ALL CAPS WITH (( )) FOR ASSOC REF*
LOCATIONS	ADD GEO LOCATION DATA TO THE LOCATIONS TAB
DATE FIRST INFO	DATE OF INFO FROM RE-PORT, USE THE CALENDAR TO SELECT DATE
DATE LAST MODIFIED	AUTOMATICALLY FILLED IN
SYMBOL CODE	AUTOMATICALLY FILLED IN
AFFILIATION	DROP DOWN SELECTION FOR AFFILIATION
ALLEGIANCE	DROP DOWN SELECTION FOR COUNTRY
INTELLIGENCE EVALUATION	DROP DOWN SELECTION FOR CONDITION
CONDITION	DROP DOWN SELECTION FOR CONDITION
SECURITY INFO	AUTOMATICALLY FILLED IN

MECHANIC SHOP ((MARUF))
(DCGSIOP-KAF9:TED)

Name	MECHANIC SHOP ((MARUF))
Locations	41RQR5300012367
Date First Info	29 0000Z Nov 2009
Date Last Modified	01 0754Z Dec 2009
Symbol Code	SSGPI----H*AF*
Affiliation	Suspect
Allegiance	AFGHANISTAN
Country	AFGHANISTAN
Intelligence Evaluation	Confirmed
Condition	Ready / Good

ATGHAR ((DISTRICT))
(DCGSIOP-KAF9:TED)

Name	ATGHAR ((DISTRICT))
Locations	42RUA4653610395
Date First Info	30 0800Z Nov 2009
Date Last Modified	30 1434Z Nov 2009
Symbol Code	OOLP--------"*G
Affiliation	None Specified
Allegiance	AFGHANISTAN
Intelligence Evaluation	Confirmed

Organization Entity

PROPERTY FIELD	STANDARD
NAME	ALL CAPS WITH (( )) FOR ASSOC REF*
LOCATIONS	ADD GEO LOCATION DATA TO THE LOCATIONS TAB
DATE FIRST INFO	DATE OF INFO FROM REPORT, USE THE CALENDAR TO SELECT DATE
DATE LAST MODIFIED	AUTOMATICALLY FILLED IN
SYMBOL CODE	AUTOMATICALLY FILLED IN
AFFILIATION	DROP DOWN SELECTION FOR AFFILIATION
ALLEGIANCE	DROP DOWN SELECTION FOR COUNTRY
NATIONALITY	DROP DOWN SELECTION FOR COUNTRY
ETHNICITY	DROP DOWN SELECTION FOR ETHNICITY, CAN BE LEFT BLANK
RELIGION	DROP DOWN SELECTION FOR RELIGION
INTELLIGENCE EVALUATION	DROP DOWN SELECTION FOR EVALUATION
THREAT LEVEL	DROP DOWN SELECTION FOR THREAT LEVEL, CAN BE LEFT BLANK
SECURITY INFO	AUTOMATICALLY FILLED IN

Person Entity

PROPERTY FIELD	STANDARD
NAME (FIRST MIDDLE LAST)	AUTOMATICALLY FILLED IN FROM NAME FIELDS BELOW
FIRST NAME	ALL CAPS FOR NAMES, USE FNU, DO NOT USE UNKNOWN
MIDDLE NAME	ALL CAPS FOR NAMES, USE MNU, DO NOT USE UNKNOWN
LAST NAME	ALL CAPS FOR NAMES, USE LNU, DO NOT USE UNKNOWN
PREFIX	FREETEXT: HONORIFIC TITLES (HAJI, MULLAH, USTAD, etc.)
SUFFIX	FREETEXT: JPEL # OR BDE TGT #, CAN BE LEFT BLANK
PRIMARY CITIZENSHIP	DROP DOWN SELECTION FOR COUNTRY
SECONDARY CITIZENSHIP	DROP DOWN SELECTION FOR COUNTRY, CAN BE BLANK
NATIONALITY	DROP DOWN SELECTION FOR COUNTRY
LOCATIONS	ADD GEO LOCATION DATA TO THE LOCATIONS TAB
DATE FIRST INFO	DATE OF INFO FROM REPORT, USE THE CALENDAR TO SELECT DATE

NATIONAL DEFENSE SERVICE ((KANDAHAR))
(DCGSIOP-KAF9:TED)

Name	NATIONAL DEFENSE SERVICE...
Locations	41RQR5300012367
Date First Info	29 0000Z Nov 2009
Date Last Modified	30 1336Z Nov 2009
Symbol Code	OAGPA-------""G
Affiliation	Assumed Friend
Allegiance	AFGHANISTAN
Nationality	AFGHANISTAN
Ethnicity	Pashtun
Religion	Muslim - Nation of Islam
Intelligence Evaluation	Possible
Threat Level	Low

FNU MNU ((LNU))
(DCGSIOP-KAF9:TED)

Name (First Middle Last)	FNU MNU ((LNU))
First Name	FNU
Middle Name	MNU
Last Name	((LNU))
Prefix	HAJI
Suffix	IS0361
Primary Citizenship	AFGHANISTAN
Secondary Citizenship	
Nationality	AFGHANISTAN
Locations	41RQR5402311055
Date First Info	29 0000Z Nov 2009

Person Entity (Continued)	
PROPERTY FIELD	**STANDARD**
DATE LAST MODIFIED	AUTOMATICALLY FILLED IN
SYMBOL CODE	AUTOMATICALLY FILLED IN
AFFILIATION	DROP DOWN SELECTION FOR AFFILIATION
ETHNICITY	DROP DOWN SELECTION FOR ETHNICITY, CAN BE BLANK
GENDER	DROP DOWN SELECTION FOR GENDER
RELIGION	DROP DOWN SELECTION FOR RELIGION
INTELLIGENCE EVALUATION	DROP DOWN SELECTION FOR EVALUATION
SECURITY INFO	AUTOMATICALLY FILLED IN

Event Entity	
PROPERTY FIELD	STANDARD
NAME	ALL CAPS WITH (( )) FOR ASSOC REF*
LOCATIONS	ADD GEO LOCATION DATA TO THE LOCATIONS TAB
DATE FIRST INFO	DATE OF INFO FROM REPORT, USE THE CALENDAR TO SELECT DATE
DATE LAST MODIFIED	AUTOMATICALLY FILLED IN
SYMBOL CODE	AUTOMATICALLY FILLED IN
AFFILIATION	DROP DOWN SELECTION FOR AFFILIATION
ALLEGIANCE	DROP DOWN SELECTION FOR COUNTRY
COUNTRY	DROP DOWN SELECTION FOR COUNTRY
PURPOSE	FREETEXT: ADDITIONAL DESCRIPTION
NATIONALITY	DROP DOWN SELECTION FOR COUNTRY
INTELLIGENCE EVALUATION	DROP DOWN SELECTION FOR EVALUATION
SECURITY INFO	AUTOMATICALLY FILLED IN

FNU MNU ((LNU))
(DCGSIOP-KAF9:TED)

Name (First Middle Last)	FNU MNU ((LNU))
First Name	FNU
Middle Name	MNU
Last Name	((LNU))
Date Last Modified	30 1340Z Nov 2009
Symbol Code	OAPPA-------**G
Affiliation	Assumed Friend
Allegiance	AFGHANISTAN
Ethnicity	Pashtun
Gender	Male
Religion	Muslim - Nation of Islam
Intelligence Evaluation	Confirmed

NOTE: the parenthetical reference will be used to identify a PERSON ENTITY Surname or Last Name. If the last name is Unknown, the (()) are still used.

STOLEN VEHICLE ((ARGHISTAN))
(DCGSIOP-KAF9:TED)

Name	STOLEN VEHICLE ((ARGHISTAN))
Locations	41RQR5404311367
Date First Info	29 0000Z Nov 2009
Date Last Modified	01 0050Z Dec 2009
Symbol Code	OOEPA-------**G
Affiliation	None Specified
Allegiance	AFGHANISTAN
Purpose	POSS VEHICLE ACQUISTION...
Nationality	AFGHANISTAN
Intelligence Evaluation	Possible

Financial Transaction Entity $

PROPERTY FIELD	STANDARD
NAME	ALL CAPS WITH (( )) FOR ASSOC REF*
LOCATIONS	ADD GEO LOCATION DATA TO THE LOCATIONS TAB
DATE FIRST INFO	DATE OF INFO FROM REPORT, USE THE CALENDAR TO SELECT DATE
DATE LAST MODIFIED	AUTOMATICALLY FILLED IN
SYMBOL CODE	AUTOMATICALLY FILLED IN
AFFILIATION	DROP DOWN SELECTION FOR AFFILIATION
ALLEGIANCE	DROP DOWN SELECTION FOR COUNTRY
PURPOSE	FREETEXT: ADDITIONAL DESCRIPTION
NATIONALITY	DROP DOWN SELECTION FOR COUNTRY

Financial Transaction Entity (Continued)

PROPERTY FIELD	STANDARD
INTELLIGENCE EVALUATION	DROP DOWN SELECTION FOR EVALUATION
DESTINATION NAME	FREETEXT: ALL CAPS, USE STATED NAMES OR NONE SPECIFIED
SOURCE COUNTRY	DROP DOWN SELECTION FOR COUNTRY
PAYMENT METHOD	DROP DOWN FOR PAYMENT METHOD
TRANSACTION TYPE	DROP DOWN FOR TRANSAC-TION TYPE
AMOUNT	FREETEXT: NUMERICAL VALUE ONLY; NO SYMBOLS
CURRENCY	DROP DOWN SELECTION FOR CURRENCY; AFGHANI
SECURITY INFO	AUTOMATICALLY FILLED IN

$ DELIVERY OF FUNDS ((SPIN BOLDAK))
(DCGSIOP-KAF9:TED)

Name	DELIVERY OF FUNDS ((SPIN BOLDAK))
Locations	41RQR5404311367
Date First Info	30 0400Z Nov 2009
Date Last Modified	01 1243Z Dec 2009
Symbol Code	OOEPA-------**G
Affiliation	None Specified
Allegiance	AFGHANISTAN
Purpose	INTENDED PAYMENT FOR SUPPLIES
Nationality	AFGHANISTAN

$ DELIVERY OF FUNDS ((SPIN BOLDAK))
(DCGSIOP-KAF9:TED)

Name	DELIVERY OF FUNDS ((SPIN BOLDAK))
Locations	41RQR5404311367
Intelligence Evaluation	Confirmed
Destination Name	NONE SPECIFIED
Source Country	PAKISTAN
Destination Country	AFGHANISTAN
Payment Method	Courier
TransactionType	Payment
Amount	100000
Currency	Afghani
SecurityInfo	

Chapter 18

Common Property Standards

18-1. Common Properties.

These common properties for entities are also standardized according to the following rules.

- ADDRESS
- COMMUNICATIONS
- ALIAS
- CRIMINAL HISTORY
- SKILLS
- REMARKS

Address Property

PROPERTY FIELD	STANDARD
ADDRESS NAME	FREETEXT: ALL CAPS; REFERENCE THE ADDRESS
CITY	FREETEXT: ALL CAPS; USE VILLAGE/CITY NAMES, CAN BE BLANK
COUNTY/PARISH	FREETEXT: USE ALL CAPS; USE DISTRICT NAMES
STATE/PROVINCE	FREETEXT: USE ALL CAPS; USE PROVINCE NAMES
COUNTRY	DROP DOWN SELECTION FOR COUNTRY
DATE LAST MODIFIED	AUTOMATICALLY FILLED IN

Addresses	1/1
Address Name	SUPPLIES DISTRIBUTED FROM
City	GHUNDI KALAY
County/Parish	ATGHAR
State/Province	ZABUL
Country	AFGHANISTAN
Date Last Modified	01 1925Z Dec 2009

Communications Property

PROPERTY FIELD	STANDARD
TYPE	DROP DOWN SELECTION FOR TYPE
PHONE NUMBER	FREETEXT: ALL NUMBERS
COUNTRY	DROP DOWN SELECTION FOR COUNTRY
DATE LAST MODIFIED	AUTOMATICALLY FILLED IN

Communications	1/1
Type	CELL PHONE NUMBER
Phone Number	((93712345678))
Country	AFGHANISTAN
Date Last Modified	02 0823Z Dec 2009

Alias Property

PROPERTY FIELD	STANDARD
ALIAS	FREETEXT: ALL CAPS, NICKNAMES, CALLSIGNS, ADDITIONAL TITLES
DATE LAST MODIFIED	AUTOMATICALLY FILLED IN

Aliases	1/1
Alias	MULLAH AGHA
Date Last Modified	01 1925Z Dec 2009

Criminal History Property

PROPERTY FIELD	STANDARD
NAME	FREETEXT: ALL CAPS; REFERENCE THE ARREST; UNKNOWN IS THE DEFAULT
INFRACTION	FREETEXT: ALL CAPS; SHORT DESCRIPTION, CAN BE BLANK
ARRESTING ORGANIZATION	FREETEXT: ALL CAPS; SHORT DESCRIPTION, CAN BE BLANK
DATE OF ARREST	DATE OF ARREST FROM REPORT, USE THE CALENDAR TO SELECT DATE
BOOK NUMBER	DROP DOWN SELECTION FOR COUNTRY
ARREST TYPE	AUTOMATICALLY FILLED IN
DESCRIPTION	FREETEXT: ALL CAPS; DESCRIPTION FROM THE REPORT
JAIL TIME (MONTHS)	FREETEXT: NUMBERS ONLY; ENTER '0' FOR LESS THAN ONE MONTH, LEAVE BLANK FOR NO JAIL TIME
DATE LAST MODIFIED	AUTOMATICALLY FILLED IN

Criminal History 1/1
Name	DETENTION AT TCP 21
Infraction	SUSPECTED SMUGGLING
Arresting Organization	AFGHAN NATIONAL POLICE
Date of Arrest	20 1000Z Sep 2009
Book Number	NONE SPECIFIED
Arrest Type	Detained
Description	SEVERAL BAGS OF FERTILIZER
Jail Time (Months)	0
Date Last Modified	02 0848Z Dec 2009

NOTE: Use separate entities for multiple Criminal Histories associated with one entity type

Skills Property

PROPERTY FIELD	STANDARD
SKILL DESCRIPTION	FREETEXT: ALL CAPS; DESCRIPTION OF FUNCTION OR ROLE
DATE LAST MODIFIED	AUTOMATICALLY FILLED IN

Skills 1/1
Skill Description	IED FACILITATOR
Date Last Modified	02 0848Z Dec 2009

Remarks Property

PROPERTY FIELD	STANDARD
SUBJECT	FREETEXT: ALL CAPS; THE FIRST REMARK WILL BE ANALYST BLOCK
DESCRIPTION	FREETEXT: ALL CAPS; ADDITIONAL INFORMATION BASED ON SUBJECT
DATE LAST MODIFIED	AUTOMATICALLY FILLED IN

Example 1, Note analyst initials in double parenthesis

Remarks 1/2
Subject	ANALYST BLOCK
Description	2 DEC 2009 ((EFW)) 572MI
Date Last Modified	01 1925Z Dec 2009

Example 2

Remarks 2/2
Subject	PATTERN OF LIFE
Description	HOME BY 1800 EVERYDAY
Date Last Modified	02 1031Z Dec 2009

NOTE: The first Remark will always be used as an Analyst Block to establish tan audit trail for each

26 July 2009   GUERRILLA HUNTER KILLER SMARTBOOK   **18-2**

18-2. Rules for recording Analyst Block entries.

Place additional Analysts information *ABOVE previous Analysts* to allow for the most recent Analyst who worked on the Entity to be seen in the Entity Properties Window.

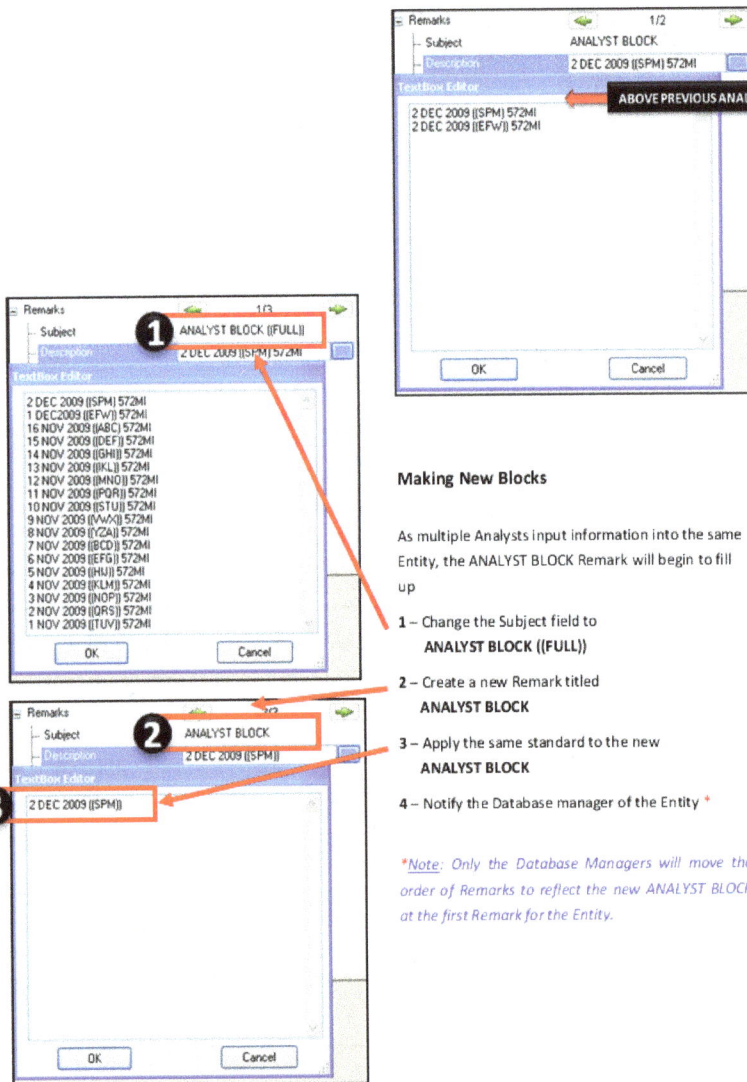

Making New Blocks

As multiple Analysts input information into the same Entity, the ANALYST BLOCK Remark will begin to fill up

1 – Change the Subject field to
   ANALYST BLOCK ((FULL))

2 – Create a new Remark titled
   ANALYST BLOCK

3 – Apply the same standard to the new
   ANALYST BLOCK

4 – Notify the Database manager of the Entity *

Note: Only the Database Managers will move the order of Remarks to reflect the new ANALYST BLOCK at the first Remark for the Entity.

Chapter 18

18-3. Settings for Entity Fields.

Set entity fields to match the following diagrams to simplify entity entry to 5/2 ID SBCT data standard.

Vehicle
Name
Skip 1
Locations
Skip 1
Date First Info
Date Last Modified
Symbol Code
Affiliation
Allegiance
Country
Skip 5
Year
Make
Model
Skip 1
License State
License County
Color
Type
Skip 3
Operational Status
Skip 9
Intelligence Eval
Security Info
Skip1
Addresses
Communications
Multimedia
Remarks
Aliases

Remarks
Subject
Description
Date Last Modified
Skip 3

Equipment
Name
Skip 2
Locations
Skip 2
Date First Info
Date Last Modified
Symbol Code
Affiliation
Allegiance
Country
Skip 5
Operational Status
Skip 1
Intelligence Eval
Skip 9
Security Info
Skip1
Addresses
Communications
Multimedia
Remarks
Aliases

Criminal History
Name
Infraction
Skip 1
Arresting Org
Date of Arrest
Book Number
Skip 2
Description
Skip 1
Jail Time (Months)
Date Last Modified
Skip 3

Event
Name
Skip 2
Locations
Skip 3
Date First Info
Date Last Modified
Symbol Code
Affiliation
Allegiance
Purpose
Nationality
Intelligence Eval
Skip 1
Security Info
Addresses
Multimedia
Communications
Remarks
Aliases

Address
Address Name
Skip 4
City
County/Parish
State/Province
Country
Skip 1
Date Last Modified
Skip 3

Organization
Name
Skip 1
Locations
Skip 1
Date First Info
Date Last Modified
Symbol Code
Affiliation
Allegiance
Skip 2
Nationality
Ethnicity
Religion
Skip 3
Intelligence Eval
Threat Level
Security Info
Skip 1
Communications
Addresses
Multimedia
Remarks
Skip 1
Skills

Multimedia
Name
File Name
Multimedia Type
Skip 1
Date Last Modified
Skip 3
File Link

Place
Name
Skip 2
Date Founded
Date First Info
Date Last Modified
Symbol Code
Affiliation
Allegiance
Intelligence Eval
Security Info
Multimedia
Addresses
Aliases
Remarks

Facility
Name
Skip 2
Locations
Skip 3
Date First Info
Date Last Modified
Symbol Code
Affiliation
Allegiance
Skip 1
Country
Activity
Confidence Status
Intelligence Eval
Condition
Skip 16
Security Info
Dimension
Addresses
Multimedia
Remarks
Aliases
Skip 2
Communications

Financial Transaction
Name
Skip 2
Locations
Date Begin
Date End
Skip 1
Date First Info
Date Last Modified
Symbol Code
Affiliation
Allegiance
Purpose
Skip 1
Nationality
Intelligence Eval
Source Name
Destination Name
Source Country
Destination Country
Payment Method
Transaction Type
Amount
Currency
Security Info
Communications
Aliases
Addresses
Multimedia
Remarks

Unit
Unit Identification
Unit Number
Unit Org Type
Unit Echelon
Locations
Skip 1
Date First Info
Date Last Modified
Symbol Code
Affiliation
Allegiance
Skip 2
Current Strength (%)
Combat Effectiveness
Country
Intelligence Eval
Skip 2
Operational Status
Skip 5
Unit Functional Role
Track Number
Skip 1
Unit Type
Skip 2
Parent Unit ID
Parent Unit Number
Parent Unit Echelon
Parent Unit Org
Parent Unit Function
Skip 3
Security Info
Multimedia
Remarks
Addresses
Aliases

UNCLASSIFIED

18-4. Persistent Jabber Chat.
The ACE maintains two persistent Jabber/PSI chat rooms for
discussion and finding help.

   a. To join, open 'service discovery' from the Jabber main menu. A window opens listing
available services. Click on 'Public Chat rooms'. The top two rooms are 5BCT's persistent intelligence chat areas.

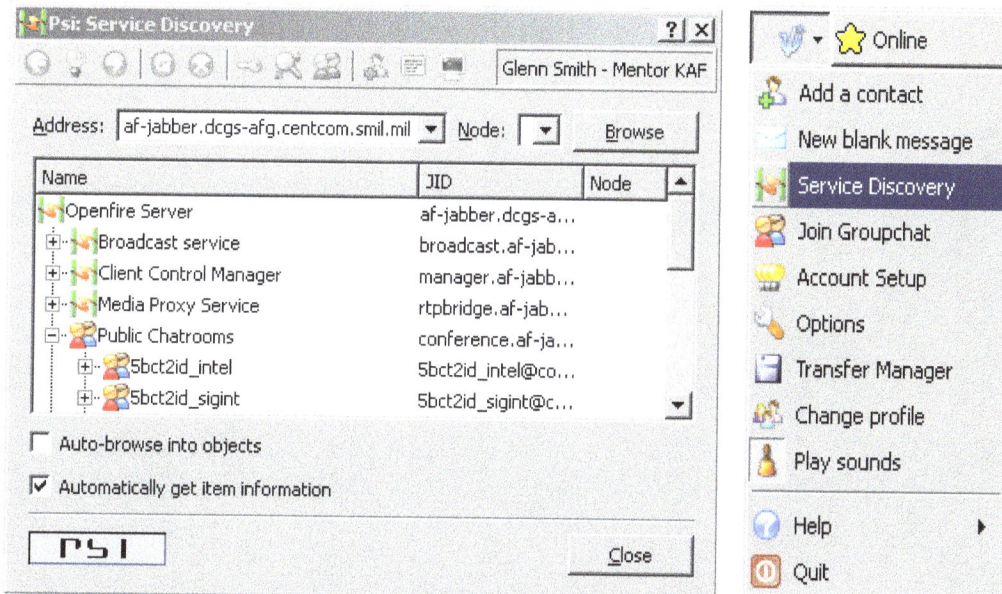

This page intentionally left blank.

Source Notes

These are the sources used, quoted, or paraphrased in this publication.

[1]FM 7-100.4. *Opposing Force Organization Guide.* May 2007. While the name and basic organization come from FM 7-100.4, the author understands that guerrilla organizations come in various shapes and sizes. Therefore several other texts were consulted in order to form the generic template. Other sources that aided in the building of the template are; NGIC publication: *Afghanistan: Opposing Militany Forces (OMF), Tactics, Techniques and Procedures, Guerilla Warfare* by Ernesto "Che" Guevera, *The Mini-Manual of the Urban Guerrilla* by Carlos Marighella, *The Handbook for Volunteers of the Irish Republican Army*, and *Mao Tse Tung on Guerrilla Warfare* by Mao Tse Tung, translated by Brigadier General Samuel B. Griffith.

[2]FM 31-21. *Guerrilla Warfare.* May 1955.

[3]FM 31-21. *Guerrilla Warfare.* May 1955.

[4]FM 7-100.4. *Opposing Force Organization Guide.* May 2007. Ernesto "Che" Guevara defined a "Column" as 100-150 personnel in *Guerrilla Warfare.* Mao Tse Tung outlined a "Company" as 36-72 personnel in *Mao Tse Tung on Guerrilla Warfare*, translated by Brigadier General Samuel B. Griffith.

[5]FM 7-100.4. *Opposing Force Organization Guide.* May 2007. Ernesto "Che" Guevara defined a "Platoon" as 30-40 personnel in *Guerrilla Warfare.* Mao Tse Tung outlined a "Platoon" as 18-36 personnel in *Mao Tse Tung on Guerrilla Warfare*, translated by Brigadier General Samuel B. Griffith. *The Handbook for Volunteers of the Irish Republican Army* describes a "Flying Column" as 15-25 personnel and Carlos Marighella outlines a "Firing Team" being 10-12 individuals in *The Mini-Manual for the Urban Guerrilla.*

[6]FM 7-100.4. *Opposing Force Organization Guide.* May 2007. FM 7-100.4. *Opposing Force Organization Guide.* May 2007. Ernesto "Che" Guevara defined a "Squad" as 8-12 personnel in *Guerrilla Warfare.* Mao Tse Tung outlined a "Squad" as 9-11 personnel in *Mao Tse Tung on Guerrilla Warfare*, translated by Brigadier General Samuel B. Griffith. *The Handbook for Volunteers of the Irish Republican Army* describes a "Section" as five personnel and Carlos Marighella outlines a "Firing Group" being 4-5 individuals in *The Mini-Manual for the Urban Guerrilla.*

[7]In *Guerrilla Warfare*, by Ernesto "Che" Guevara states that, "in guerrilla warfare, the squad is the functional unit."

[8]Carlos Marighella in *The Mini-Manual of the Urban Guerrilla* says, "the firing group (4-5 Personnel) plans and executes urban guerrilla actions, obtains and stores weapons, and studies and corrects its own tactics. When there are tasks planned by the strategic command, these tasks take preference. But there is no such thing as a firing group without its own initiative." *The Handbook for Volunteers of the Irish Republican Army* also emphasizes initiative, stating that the Column (15-25 Personnel) "Operationally, it is under higher command but at the same time knows its own field of operations and carries out its tasks without further checking. It may be called on by higher command to carry out certain tasks or support other columns in the field, but most if its time will be taken up with local operations."

[9]The idea of guerrilla forces further extending their control of the local populace comes from FM 31-21. *Guerrilla Warfare.* May 1955, and *Mao Tse Tung on Guerrilla Warfare* by Mao Tse Tung, translated by Brigadier General Samuel B. Griffith.

[10]Ernesto "Che" Guevara made constant references to "contacts" that aided in their guerrilla movement during the Revolution. These "contacts" were sometimes committed members of the Revolutionary Movement, or simply peasants that provided key functions for the guerrillas. *Episodes of the Cuban Revolutionary War, 1956-1958* by Ernesto "Che" Guevara.

[11]Ernesto "Che" Guevara describes the civil organization in *Guerrilla Warfare.* "Che" goes on to describe the civil organization of the insurrectional movement existing on two fronts; internal and external. "Che" defines the internal front being in a "place dominated, relatively speaking, by the forces of liberation," whereas the external front is in a "zone penetrated by the enemy."

[12]In *Guerrilla Warfare*, Ernesto "Che" Guevara outlines the "Beginning, development, and end of a guerrilla war" as beginning in a certain zone. Once that zone is under full guerrilla control, the guerrilla movement continues to expand as more and more support is gained into zones not under full control.

[13]Because "Che" Guevara continually makes reference to the battlefield as zones in *Guerrilla Warfare*, the author sought to define what these zones might look like for the Guerrilla Hunter Killer. The term "Zone of Operation" comes directly from *Guerrilla Warfare* while FM 31-21. *Guerrilla Warfare.* May 1955 provided a starting point for the GH/K Zone of Operations with the "Area not controlled effectively by either force."

[14]FM 31-21. *Guerrilla Warfare.* May 1955. "Area controlled effectively by guerrillas."

[15]FM90-8. Counter Guerrilla Operations. August 1986.

[16]FM90-8. Counter Guerrilla Operations. August 1986.

Source Notes

[17]FM 31-21. *Guerrilla Warfare.* May 1955. "Area controlled effectively by the enemy." The term "Zone of Security" comes from *Guerrilla Warfare* by Ernesto "Che" Guevara. While "Che" never gives a definition for the "Zone of Security" he does state that the range of a guerrilla band will be limited "by the time it takes to arrive at a zone of security from the zone of operations," and the necessity to "maintain stable lines of communication," thus the GH/K Zone of Security was created.

[18]All definitions for this chapter were taken exclusively from FM 7-100.1. *Opposing Force Operations.* December 2004.

[19]All definitions for this chapter were taken exclusively from FM 7-100.1. *Opposing Force Operations.* December 2004.

[20]Carlos Marighella in, *Minimanual of the Urban Guerrilla* describes "liberation of prisoners" as one of the fourteen types of missions for the Urban Guerrilla. Marighella goes on to describe "jails of the enemy as the inevitable site of guerrilla actions designed to liberate his ideological comrades from prison. It is this combination of the urban guerrilla in freedom and the urban guerrilla in jail that results in the armed operations we refer to as liberation of prisoners."

[21]One of the key tenants of Guerrilla Warfare is the Guerrilla must live to fight another day, because of this the Guerrilla will take all measures necessary to ensure not only a successful attack, but a even more successful withdrawal. In *Guerrilla Warfare,* Ernesto "Che" Guevara describes controlling guerrilla "paths of escape" and enemy "roads of access" with guards and well planned ambushes. "Che" also describes the mine as the "best and surest weapon against the tank." He also goes on to recommend the use of "sloping ditches" as a defense against tanks. The author adapted these points to outline how the GH/K would ensure his withdrawal during a Defense to Preserve.

Glossary

The glossary lists acronyms and terms with Army, multi-service, or joint definitions, and other selected terms. Where Army and Joint definitions are different, *(Army)* follows the term. The proponent manual for other terms is listed in parentheses after the definition.

SECTION I - ACRONYMS AND ABBREVIATIONS

GH/K	guerrilla hunter killer
EGH/K C2	external guerilla hunter killer command and control
EGH/KCO	external guerrilla hunter killer civil organization
IGH/K C2	internal guerrilla hunter killer command and control
IGH/KCO	internal guerrilla hunter killer civil organization

SECTION II - TERMS AND DEFINITIONS

Base Camp Zone

This zone is effectively controlled by the Guerrilla Hunter Killer. Headquarters and base camps will be located in this zone, usually in difficult terrain. Limited defensive operations will be conducted in this zone against enemy forces seeking to penetrate this zone.

External Guerrilla Hunter Killer Command and Control

External GH/K C2 (EGH/K C2) is part of the GH/K structure but is not located within the principal GH/K Macro Zones, but is instead located in a neighboring country or state not actively involved in GH/K Operations. External GH/K C2 will develop the left and right limits of GH/K operations and organization along with issuing broad guidance to Internal GH/K C2. External GH/K C2 will supply Internal GH/K C2 with supplies not readily available within the principal GH/K zones. An example of this in Afghanistan would be the Taliban Senior Leadership (TBSL). The TBSL is located in neighboring Pakistan, but still issue broad orders and guidance to tactical level commanders in the form of directives, as well as providing supplies not easily found within Afghanistan commanders.

Glossary

External Guerrilla Hunter Killer Civil Organization

The External Guerrilla Hunter Killer Civil Organization (EGH/KCO) is found in the Zone of Security and Operations. The EGH/KCO performs many of the same functions as the IGH/KCO but is nowhere near as robust as the IGH/KCO because these zones are not under full GH/K control.

Internal Guerrilla Hunter Killer Command and Control

Internal GH/K C2 (IGH/K C2) comes from GH/K units located in the principal GH/K Macro Zones. The internal GH/K C2 acts independently with minimal guidance from the External GH/K C2. When given a specific task by the External GH/K C2 this task will take preference, otherwise the Internal GH/K C2 displays its own initiative by planning and executing their own actions along with the procurement of logistics easily obtainable in zone. In Afghanistan, Internal Guerrilla Hunter Killer Command and Control is exercised by the tactical level commanders.

Internal Guerrilla Hunter Killer Civil Organization

The Internal Guerrilla Hunter Killer Civil Organization (IGH/KCO) is found in the GH/K Base Camp Zone. The IGH/KCO is emplaced to efficiently govern the local populace and influence the people to the GH/K's side. The functions of the internal IGH/KCO can include, but are not limited to collection of taxes, establishment of a penal code and civil code along with the establishment of a judicial system to settle local disputes and enforce punishment on the local population for failure to follow the established IGH/KCO laws. The IGH/KCO will also establish regulations for the population to contribute food and other necessary supplies to the GH/K. There will always be a strong propaganda element to the IGH/KCO IOT explain to the population the reasons for the implementation of taxes and laws. This propaganda will also show how the legitimate government is not providing the basic civil functions where as the IGH/KCO is. Through this propaganda the GH/K will be able to exploit their success amongst the local population in other zones enabling the further penetration of the GH/K for the GH/K's success lies in the support of the people.

Guerrilla Hunter Killer Base Camp

Located within the Base Camp Zone, GH/K Base Camps house command posts, training areas, communications facilities, medical stations, and logistics centers. The Guerrilla Hunter Killer can defend or attack out of his GH/K base camp. However, it is important to note that the GH/K does not seek to defend these base camps for any length of time; therefore he does not.

Guerrilla Hunter Killer Camp

The GH/K camp is a small temporary position employed by the GH/K in the Zone of Security in route to the Zone of Operations or Base Camp Zone. The GH/K camp is employed for resting of forces, intermediate C2 or sudden meetings of GH/K leadership.

Guerrilla Hunter Killer Company

The GH/K Company has anywhere from 77-101 personnel comprised of 3 GH/K Groups and a Headquarters and Command element. The GH/K Company Headquarters and Command element is responsible for providing command and control as well as logistical support for GH/K Group operations. The GH/K Company is assessed to exist at the District level in RC(S).

Guerrilla Hunter Killer Group

GH/K Groups will have anywhere from 18-27 personnel comprised of three GH/K Teams and a Headquarters and Command element. The GH/K Company Headquarters and Command element is responsible for providing command and control as well as logistical support for GH/K Team operations.

Guerrilla Hunter Killer Macro Zones

The primary mission of the Guerrilla Hunter Killer is to continually expand his control over a country or state. In order to accomplish this mission the battlefield can view from a Macro level as comprising three primary zones. Each zone performs a specific function to the Guerrilla Hunter Killer and are necessary to expand his control. Defining and understanding the battlefield using these zones can be used as a very effective metric for maneuver forces.

Guerrilla Hunter Killer Micro Zones

The Guerrilla Hunter Killer Micro Zones exist within the Macro Zones. The Micro Zones exist in both the offense and defense. The Micro Zones are the Battle, Attack, Kill, Disruption and Forward Support Zones.

Guerrilla Hunter Killer Militia

Civilians, organized and committed to an active part of the Guerrilla Hunter Killer movement. The size of the GH/K Militia will vary depending on the size of their respective village, but the GH/K Militia will be structurally as close to GH/K main forces organization as possible, and will not exceed typical GH/K Group size.

Glossary

Guerrilla Hunter Killer Team

The GH/K Team is the most effective unit in the Guerrilla Hunter Killer formation and the most commonly seen unit on the battlefield. The GH/K Team recognizes it is subordinate to the GH/K Group and will execute direct orders from the GH/K Group but mostly the GH/K Team will operate under its own initiative. This includes selecting their own targets and being responsible for basic logistical needs. A member of the GH/K Team may be assigned more than one role in the Team. For example a specific mission may not call for the Grenadier to employ his RPG or ammunition for the RPG may not be available, therefore he may take on the role of Surveillance for the GH/K Team.

Zone of Security

This zone is not controlled effectively by either the Guerrilla Hunter Killer or the enemy. This is the principal transient area used by the GH/K to reach the Zone of Operations. The GH/K will not offer determined resistance to the enemy in this zone for he wishes to keep this zone open in order to maintain freedom of maneuver from the Base Camp Zone to the Zone of Operations and vice versa. The GH/K will conduct limited harassing type attacks to limit enemy movement in the zone.

Zone of Operations

This is the principal zone of GH/K operations, as it is somewhat effectively controlled by the enemy. GH/K's seek to bring more of this zone under effective control. The Zone of Operations can further be divided into the Guerrilla Hunter Killer Micro (below) zones among the subordinate GH/K units. Within these areas each subordinate unit exercises control over the civilian population, selects targets and carries out attacks with broad guidance from their next level of command. Occasionally the GH/K will be directed to carry out a specific attack which will take precedence, but this is not the norm.

Symbology

NAME	SYMBOL
GH/K COMPANY	
GH/K GROUP	
GH/K TEAM	
GH/K MILITIA	
EGH/KCO C2	
EGH/KCO	
IGH/KCO C2	
IGH/KCO	
GH/K CONTACT	
GH/K SURVEILLANCE	
GH/K LOGISTICS	
GH/K MEDICAL	
NARCOTICS	

Afterword

This Smartbook is not the complete answer to solving intelligence deficiencies in the Global War on Terror, nor do I claim it to be. However, I do feel it represents the first step to re-invigorating Military Intelligence across all echelons, by returning analysts back to a true intelligence. While this process was developed during our deployment to Afghanistan, the methods outlined are timeless. The process outlined in this Smartbook can be applied to any Counter-Insurgency conflict across the globe.

Numerous individuals contributed to our success as a Military Intelligence Company and to the completion of this Smartbook. I would like to thank our Embedded Support Members and DCGS-A PM SIL Members; Kevin Mullis, Chad Hultz, Tom Orlando, Andy Waldman, LTC Thomas Gloor, MAJ Ed Weakley, Shaun Cronen, Jeff Bell and Rosa Miranda for their hard work and determination to make DCGS-A work for us. SFC(P) Nicholas, Psaki, Robert "Derm" McDermott, Jeremiah Anderson, Chris Strawser, MAJ Darrell Collins, CW3 Deborah Hoover and CW3 Kathleen Mahoney all aided greatly in our efforts. I would also like to thank SSG Zachary Jaenisch for his tireless efforts to compile all of the various Microsoft Word documents and PowerPoint presentations into what became this Smartbook.

I would also like to recognize two of the finest All-Source Intelligence Technicians in the U.S Army; CW2 Tina Davis and CW2 Earl Wilson. Ms. Davis, and Mr. Wilson epitomize everything a true Intelligence Technician should and need to be. If not for their skill, innovation and determination none of our accomplishments would have been possible.

Finally, and most importantly I would like to thank all of the Soldiers, NCO's and Officers of the 572nd Military Intelligence Company, "MOJAVE", for their vigorous and often times frustrating endeavors to implement the process outlined in the Smartbook. The members of "MOJAVE" Company faced numerous challenges during OEF 09-11, but the company proved themselves to be true intelligence professionals as each challenge was overcome as another presented itself. The Soldiers of "MOJAVE" Company have made ripples in the lake of Military Intelligence that will not soon be forgotten.

Sean P. Michaelson
CPT, MI
Commanding

572nd Military Intelligence Company

"Strength in intelligence, victory in war."

This page intentionally left blank.